WOLVES
in
CANADA

Erin McCloskey

LONE PINE

The Publisher: Lone Pine Publishing
10145 – 81 Avenue
Edmonton, AB T6E 1W9

Website: www.lonepinepublishing.com

Library and Archives Canada Cataloguing in Publication

McCloskey, Erin, 1970–
    Wolves in Canada / Erin McCloskey.

Includes bibliographical references.

ISBN 978-1-55105-872-6

    1. Wolves--Canada. 2. Wolves--Canada--Control. I. Title.

QL737.C22M324 2011   599.7730971   C2011-900732-0

Editorial Director: Nancy Foulds
Editorial: Kelsey Everton, Sheila Quinlan
Production Manager: Gene Longson
Book Design and Layout: Janina Kuerschner
Cover Design: Gerry Dotto
Cover Photo: Terry Parker
Maps: Volker Bodegom
Photos: Algonquin Park Museum 51; Volker Beckmann 197; Jim Butler 107, 160; Lu Carbyn 16, 68, 181; Dushenina 201; Glenbow Archives NA-5487-1 120; Lori Labrecque 40; Terry Parker 59; photos.com 10, 25, 27, 34, 55, 60, 65, 135, 136, 144, 166, 195.
Illustrations: Gary Ross, Ian Sheldon
Author Photo: Connie McCloskey

We acknowledge the financial support of the Government of Canada through the Canada Book Fund (CBF) for our publishing activities.

PC: 5

Contents

Dedication

For Grandma, with love.

And for my nephew Zack, the little man-cub who was born while this book was being written. I look forward to going out into the Canadian wilds with you someday and listening to wolves howl.

Acknowledgements

Thank you Lone Pine, especially Shane Kennedy, Nancy Foulds, Sheila Quinlan, Kelsey Everton, Volker Bodegom and Janina Kuerschner. Special thanks to Lu Carbyn for your graciousness in sharing your expertise and photographs— your life work with wolves is an inspiration. Thanks to Jim Butler for your words and images and continued mentorship. I acknowledge with appreciation the assistance provided from the biologists and wildlife experts at each of the Fish and Wildlife agencies who answered my many questions. Thanks also to Malik Awan, Julie Ross, Chris Hotson, Volker Beckmann, Friends of Algonquin Provincial Park, Fur Council of Canada, Y2Y Conservation Initiative, Defenders of Wildlife, International Wolf Centre and the IUCN/SCC Canid Specialist Group. Thank you, Mom, for every newspaper clipping and your concerned watch on the wolves and all wildlife; thank you, Dad, for being pro-coyote and anti-poison on your land. Thanks to all of you in Canada who raise your voices in support of wolf and wilderness con-servation—to all of you whose spirits run with the wolves.

Foreword

The first European settlers arrived in North America in the early part of the 17th century. They encountered a vast landscape, thinly populated by First Nations peoples and richly endowed with nature and its bountiful components. Within four centuries, humanity has dramatically changed the landscape. Most of North America has been fished, furred, logged, ploughed, dammed, paved and peopled. Fragmented habitats, forests and grasslands are ever diminishing in size and quality. These areas are small vestiges of what once were contiguous ecosystems that were important areas for large carnivores and their native prey species. Green spaces are now protected as special natural reserves, national parks and state and provincial forest reserves.

Wolves, the largest of the canids, were once widespread, but their range has been greatly reduced. Wolves can get along well with people—as long as they are not persecuted, which becomes difficult when competition with man comes into play. Wolves eat meat and so do humans. Ranchers and farmers raise cattle for domestic use and wolves do not distinguish between cows and elk: both are fair game. Wolves also compete with hunters when human hunting pressures are high, which means that, with over four centuries of persecution by man, nearly all the wolves in the United States have been eliminated. However, in Canada, the northern portion of its range, the species continues to thrive...

Research initiatives about the species began in Alaska, when Adolph Murie published his seminal monograph on wolves in 1944. It was the first time that a scientist had looked at the species in an objective way and evaluated its role within the large mammal community in a wilderness setting. Canada's first contribution to objective wolf research came a few years later, when Douglas Pimlott from the University of Toronto carried out wolf studies in Algonquin Provincial Park, Ontario. By 2011, many universities have extensive research programs on wolves. Naturalistic studies of earlier times have been overtaken by very sophisticated studies using satellite tracking, iridium, two-way links, GPS storage, data downloading, activity sensors, metadata tagging and much more. Some biologists have even graduated with degrees in science studying the ecology of wolves without ever having seen a wolf in the wild. Such are the changes over relatively a brief period of time.

Much of the current research on wolves is being carried out in Yellowstone National Park, located mainly in Wyoming. The wolves in Yellowstone are not native wolves but Canadian wolves that were reintroduced to the area after an absence of about 50 years. The program has generated much heated debate and controversy. Many agencies and individuals have spent an enormous amount of time and resources on the project. Reintroduction ideas were first debated in the 1950s. After extensive public hearings, with much support from the general public and massive opposition from the ranching community, the Americans finally decided to go ahead with the reintroduction. Wolves were still numerous in nearby Canada, which had far more open and unspoiled spaces than in the highly developed areas farther south. In 1995–96, 31 Canadian wolves were captured in Alberta and 17 in British Columbia. These, together with an additional 35 Canadian wolves, were released in Yellowstone National Park and Idaho. The program was a resounding success. The population growth rate averaged 20%, and within five years, wolves had reoccupied most of the park areas. In addition, the species extended its reach beyond park boundaries, and negatively affected some cattle ranchers who lost cows to wolf predation.

The successful reintroduction of wolves in the United States gave rise to a plethora of books about Canadian wolves in an American setting. By comparison, very few books have been written exclusively about Canadian wolves in Canada. This book by Erin McCloskey is the first that covers a pan-Canadian perspective of wolves in Canada, from coast to coast to coast. It is an extensive overview about the species itself, about its distribution, behaviour, ecology, management and conservation.

Erin McCloskey has carried out an extensive search of the literature, both popular and scientific. She has drawn from government sources, personal interviews and a detailed review of the huge literature available on the subject. This book is not peer-reviewed, but it offers something equally important—Erin's own informed perspective as a biologist and appreciator of wildlife. It is her interpretation of a species that has come under the magnifying glass, evaluating the carnivore's role in the modern world. No two people think exactly alike on all aspects of such a magnificent symbol of the wilderness as the wolf, and individual insight broadens everyone's perceptions. Erin's book has a special appeal, because her insight, reflecting her values and analysis of the records, is extremely valuable. With the meticulous insights of a scholar and biologist, Erin McCloskey has brought her interest in nature and her personal voice to a fascinating subject.

Dr. Lu Carbyn
Research Scientist Emeritus, Canadian Wildlife Service
Adjunct Professor, University of Alberta
Member of the International Union for Conservation of Nature and
Natural Resources (IUCN) Wolf Specialist Group

Preface

In 1957, my father was 18 and immigrated to Canada from Scotland. He got off the boat in Saint John, New Brunswick, and boarded the Canadian Pacific Dayliner to embark on a four-day journey across the country to Edmonton, Alberta. Those times were so different from today, when people holiday around the world without giving much thought to the distance. Dad had studied in Glasgow to be a horologist, and once he got to Edmonton, he would begin working as a watchmaker for the Hudson's Bay Company, at that time still very much retaining its frontier store persona: furs, whale oil and the iconic red, green and yellow–striped wool blankets were among the standard inventory.

Dad's journey took place in mid-February, and the cold and snow made its impression, as it always does to those who have never before experienced a Canadian winter. Dad recounts the first stop after arriving in Montreal. He got off the train to stretch his legs and smoke a cigarette on the platform. The frigid air hit him in the face and he unwittingly took a deep breath, nearly freezing his lungs. He was seized with doubt about his choice of new country—the spiders and snakes that had dissuaded him from immigrating to Australia now seemed somewhat more appealing. Soon, though, something remarkable was going to happen—an adrenaline-charged,

unforgettable event that would, like an initiation, spark the inception of his Canadian identity.

It was late at night and Dad was sitting up in the Dayliner's scenic dome, the panoramic viewing level above some of the front cars. The lights from the carriage were like a beacon in the night, casting a warm glow across the frozen fields of rocky, snowy emptiness as the train rhythmically chugged its route through the landscape. Crossing the Canadian Shield, somewhere in central Ontario, Dad stared out the window at the snow and rocks and contemplated the endlessness of this place, how the wilderness just seemed to go on forever without a trace of civilization. He was startled out of his musings by what he first thought were three or four large feral dogs. Everybody in the carriage looked and somebody exclaimed, "That's wolves!" A pack of large wolves had come charging out of the nearby woodlands, seemingly just for the fun of racing the train. Dad recalls how they blasted alongside the train, their long legs reaching ahead in an easy lope though the train must have been moving about 50 km per hour. The wolves raced alongside the train for some distance before they tore off out of sight, veering out of the orange glow of the artificial light and into the darkness. Now this, my dad acknowledged, is Canada. Ten years later, the Canadian mint stamped its centennial coin (1867–1967) with a howling wolf.

It is a quintessentially iconic Canadian image, the most wild of wilderness events to behold: wild wolves running in the night. How many Canadians today have seen a wolf in the wild? Have heard its howl? Even if they have never seen or heard a wild wolf, do Canadians value the wolf's existence in Canada? I believe most Canadians would answer, and have answered, "Yes."

This book is neither a field guide nor a glossy photographic celebration of a charismatic species. This book is in recognition of an icon of the Canadian wilderness: the wolf. It is also in recognition of Canadians who see their own Canadian identity—one that is always seeking validation—as an identity shared with and intrinsically connected to Canadian wilderness and the species that have captured our imaginations and respect. Extirpated from most of North America, the wolf is now primarily a Canadian species. A handful of the animals remain just south of our border and Alaska sustains a significant population, but the range map of the wolf in North America (see p. 12) shows that the wolf is undeniably a Canadian species.

Not ignoring the past persecution or the persecution the wolf still endures, we will ask why the wolf has thrived so well within the embrace of the Canadian border. Perhaps we can remind ourselves, recognize and acknowledge that wilderness is integral to the Canadian identity—just as my father did half a century ago.

Pre-European and Current North America Wolf Range

* Greenland's wolf range is not illustrated.

Introduction

And when, on the still cold nights, he pointed his nose at a star and howled long and wolflike, it was his ancestors, dead and dust, pointing nose at star and howling down through the centuries and through him.

–Jack London, Call of the Wild

I am a child of the prairies, where coyotes are more common than wolves. Coyotes yipped and howled me to sleep at night throughout my childhood—elsewhere, other Canadian children were hearing wolves howl. What messages were those kids getting about wolves from their parents, their elders, their neighbours, their teachers? What messages do they get today? Do they differ? Most Canadian kids receive an innate joy from seeing wild animals and value wild areas where imaginations can also run wild.

Hunter education and outdoor skills were taught to us in grade school alongside biology class. One of my teachers took us hiking and taught us how to identify tracks, survive in a winter lean-to and identify edible plants. Another of my teachers showed us a film on a wolf extermination program. I don't recall if it was documented in the US or Canada or even my home province of Alberta, but I remember it was in black and white—but all I could see was red. Hundreds of wolves were slaughtered; many men piled the bodies or posed smiling beside the carcasses. I was shocked. I had seen hunting and dead animals, seen enough wildlife documentaries and lost enough pets to predation to understand natural law. This film I was watching was not natural. It was horrific. I became an advocate for wolf conservation on that day.

Many Canadian hunters and trappers are conservationists at heart. They value wilderness and wildlife. They see themselves as a part of the system. There are valid arguments for predator control in our terribly out-of-balance natural systems. Woodland caribou are on the brink of extinction in Alberta through erroneous human exploitation—not the fault of wolves, but of course, wolves cannot understand not to hunt their natural prey base. We would like to tell them not to kill caribou, and then we would like to tell them not to kill any of our millions of head of livestock that we have filled their habitat with either. Basically, we don't want them to hunt anything that we value. With habitat loss and other environmental factors curbing prey availability, our preferences for what we would like wolves to hunt don't factor in with a hungry wolf. But wolf culls (deliberate and systematic killing of high numbers of wolves, beyond regular hunting or trapping harvests) are wrought with complications that are inherent in the very biologically evolved reproductive and behavioural strategies of wolves. The population of wolves is tied directly to prey availability. Where there is available prey for wolves, caribou and livestock included, it is we humans who don't want to be pushed out of our quotas—so we cull. But the population of the prey base will then be relatively large in proportion to the number of wolves. The remaining wolves respond to the abundance of prey and produce more pups and soon the wolf population returns to original numbers. It is an endless cycle, until we can ultimately cull industrial and urban development from our wilderness areas. Adequate habitat will allow predator-prey dynamics to be less erratic and species' populations to maintain sustainable numbers, also reducing the need for wolves to seek out domestic livestock as prey.

It is increasingly more and more important to ensure habitat protection. It is unreasonable to hope that wolves and our wildlife, in all its diversity, can survive further reduction of habitat through unsustainable farming practices, industrial development and urban sprawl.

We have read about, watched films about and still hear about the extinctions of animals, and indeed groups of native peoples, as the Europeans settled North America. Conservationists still lobby for wolf reintroductions, hunting moratoriums and habitat protection. Despite the near-complete eradication of wolves from the lower 48 of the United States, reintroduction programs to restore ecological balance to United States national parks and natural migration of Canadian wolves across the border still face hostile resistance from a great number of Americans. In Alaska wolves survive in healthy numbers, but many people want to strictly limit wolf presence, often by using inhumane methods such as poisoning or unsportsmanlike aerial shooting. These attitudes may disappear with increased public education on wildlife conservation.

In all countries where the wolf lives, wolf conservation wages a daily battle with human intolerance. Intolerance in the United States persecuted the wolf with vengeance all the way to the Medicine Line, where it had to stop dead in its own tracks. Intolerance keeps a vigilant watch at parts of that wispy man-made political borderline, and sneaks into Canada from time to time with rifles and poison, proselytizing with evangelical fervour for us to pick up our swords and slay the beast, but its voice is not effective here. This intolerance is weaker in Canada. Perhaps the wolf is stronger in our great boreal forests. Or perhaps it's simply that Canadians identify their nation as one that embraces wilderness, with the wolf embodying what we identify as truly wild. Indeed, the howl of the wolf is synonymous with "the call of the wild." Intolerance is left to watch with squinty eyes the far northern horizon, to see that iconic silhouette howling at the moon. It is a haunting, mournful call. It is also a mysterious call, understood only by the wolves, but to me it speaks of survival, defiance, joy and sorrow. The wolf seems to call out in celebration of life and in reverence to the spirits of its ancestors.

As with much of wildlife conservation history in North America, most literature about wolves references case studies of past and present situations in the United States. We are going to focus on Canada, home to the largest remaining tracts of true North American wilderness and the world's largest population of wolves. There may be conflicts and mitigation issues, but the wolf will survive and hopefully thrive in Canada. There is still so much to learn about wolves and how we can ethically and conscientiously share their space with them in Canada. But what we Canadians already know and ensure is that in the great forests and mighty Rockies, from temperate shores to remote frozen islands, on the vast plains and austere tundra, *the wolf is home.*

Natural History and Status of Canadian Wolves

Natural history can be defined as the study of a living organism's origin, evolution, relationships with other organisms, lifestyle, diet, reproduction, social grouping, behaviour, habitat, physiology and so on. These observations define an organism and differentiate it from others. Wolves evolved over thousands of years from other wolf-like animals, with each generation adapting to their environments and competing to secure ecological niches. What makes a wolf a wolf? How are wolves distinct from other dogs? Distinctions can also be made within a species, illustrating that species are dynamic and adaptable, creating subcategories such as sub-species, races, ecotypes or other descriptors to define unique populations. Hopefully, the more we learn about wolves, and learn from wolves, the wiser we will become—not only about wolf conservation, but about wildlife and wilderness conservation in general. Wolves are not homogeneous across Canada. However, as a whole, wolves are charismatic large mammals, with a population that spreads itself over much of the country, where what we describe as wilderness remains.

Ecozones of Canada

Arctic
Taiga/Tundra
Timber/Boreal
Mixedwood Plains/Maritime
Prairies
⬚ wolves absent
^^ cordillera

POPULATION

Status and Distribution

Wolves were once one of the most widely distributed mammals in the world. Today they occupy perhaps half of their former range and are extirpated from many of their former habitats. The wolf once ranged throughout North America but is now extirpated from almost all of its range south of the Canadian border, except a few northern states. Despite losing one-fifth of its former Canadian range, Canada's wolf is an estimated near 43,000 to 61,500 population stronghold of the species in North America.

Even after wolves were nearly eradicated from the lower 48 states, Canadian wolves have been making their way back across the border into Montana, Washington, New York and New England with trepidation, and were deliberately relocated by means of reintroduction programs into the northern US Rockies. In the lower United States today, there are a few grey wolf populations that exist in isolation from each other and total perhaps 2000 individuals altogether. One group is the controversial wolves in and around Yellowstone National Park and in northwestern Wyoming, extending into Montana and Idaho and now Washington and Oregon as well. These wolves have brought some ecosystem integrity to the national park that was once viewed as merely a recreation area for people, rather than a sanctuary for wildlife. Tourism has actually increased with people coming to hear the wolves howl. Another population of grey wolves is established in Minnesota, Wisconsin and the Upper Peninsula of Michigan. These two populations experience an influx of natural migration from Canada that supplements the populations, and wolves have been known to range between the United States and Canada, unobservant of political borders. Lastly, there is a remnant population of Mexican wolves (*Canis lupus bailey*) in Arizona and New Mexico, with a population count at the time of writing this book of only 42 individuals, three of which were illegally shot in the spring of 2010. The Defenders of Wildlife offered up to $10,000 for information leading to the arrest and conviction of the poacher(s). This southernmost wolf in North America is now extinct in the wild in Mexico (officially declared so sometime between 1977 and 1980). The last five wild Mexican wolves thought to be remaining were captured in Mexico and placed in captivity to establish a captive breeding program. In Alaska, the grey wolf population is approximately 7000–11,000.

The endangered red wolf of the southeastern US (with an approximate wild population of about 100) is recognized as a separate species (*Canis rufus*) from the grey wolf (*Canis lupus*). Canada is also home to the eastern wolf, which is scientifically but not yet officially designated a separate species of wolf from the grey wolf; it is closely, if not directly, related to the aforementioned red wolf. We will discuss this population, as well as the various subspecies names given to groups of wolves in Canada and the use of common names, which are often misleading, in a later section (see Taxonomy, p. 28).

Canada's population of wolves is believed to be equal to, if not greater than, the entire population of wolves in all of Eurasia. The grey wolf of Europe survives in several countries but in critically low numbers (less than 10 individuals in some countries), with most of the animals in Russia, the former Soviet Union and Mongolia. Throughout the rest of the northern hemisphere, wolves survive in populations that are low or unknown.

Wolves have adapted to an incredibly diverse array of habitats and have one of the broadest distributions of any mammal in Canada. They range coast to coast to coast—between Labrador, the Pacific Northwest and the Arctic—and beyond the mainland onto many Canadian islands. Wolves were extirpated from the Maritime islands and never lived on Prince Edward Island, but inhabit Vancouver Island and some adjacent islands (but not the Queen Charlotte Islands) and most of the arctic islands, such as Ellesmere, Baffin, Southampton,

Banks and Victoria Islands. Wolves inhabit the great boreal forest that spans the country in a continuous belt from the Labrador coast west to the Rocky Mountains and northwest to Alaska. They inhabit the Canadian Shield, the Great Plains and interior BC, above the Arctic Circle, across the northern tundra and south to the US border and beyond. The wolf skirts and flirts with that southern border, dipping its toes across the line as if it's testing the waters: in places the water is fine, in others hazardous. Indeed, some parts of the US may be safer than Canada for wolves; wolves can be shot in Canada whereas in the US (except Alaska) the wolf is a protected species (although delisting the wolf from endangered species status in the US is currently under consideration). The wolf is rarely seen near the British Columbia–US border until near the Rocky Mountains, and is largely absent from the southern Canadian prairies east of the Rocky Mountain foothills. When the wolf reaches Ontario and Quebec it disperses throughout the provinces and again tiptoes across the border into the eastern United States.

It is difficult to make population estimates for any large carnivore in Canada, owing to the animals' elusiveness, their highly mobile natures and their large home ranges. Wolves in particular are highly social, forming packs that establish hunting and breeding territories separate from other wolf packs, making them a non-cohesive species to track. As well, the terrain and climate of remote arctic regions make them difficult to study. Wolf territories may be vast, especially if prey densities are low, giving researchers the additional challenge of tracking them over large areas.

What scientists and researchers know about wolves is limited. Some populations are highly studied: the longest continuous wolf study in the world has been ongoing in Ontario's Algonquin Provincial Park since the 1950s and follows population dynamics from year to year. Conversely, the current population of wolves in the far north Arctic Archipelago is virtually unknown. Sightings confirm that arctic wolves range over most of the arctic islands as well as the mainland across all three territories, but their status is sensitive.

Predator and prey populations and densities do not see annual incremental growth but instead fluctuate over multiple years. This predator–prey dynamic illustrates a simplified cause and effect: increased prey allows a response in predator population growth, followed by increased predation and decreased prey population, and eventually the predator population reduces. Back and forth the metronome swings, but there is an entire symphony of instruments orchestrating the rhythm: climate, habitat, disease, hunting, interspecies competition. Given all these factors influencing population dynamics, surveys would have to take place every few years to be accurate, but they are too labour-intensive and time-consuming to permit. At best, population estimates are made every decade, but often from statistical models rather than field surveys. Observations made by people who live in rural communities or on acreages and ranches, or by people who spend significant time in the field hunting or trapping, can give insights into population estimates.

However, while it can be valuable, people observing wolves is an inherently erroneous source of population analysis. For example, a person reporting a wolf sighting in Glacier National Park, the US park connected to Waterton Lakes National Park in the southern Canadian Rockies, and another person sighting a wolf in Fort St. John in northern BC may be looking at the same wolf. In a 1987 study, researchers radio-tracked a wolf traversing this vast 700 km range. Radio-collaring and telemetry show how far wolves can range. Therefore, human observation is not an accurate insight into population abundance. Modern research techniques—for example, taking hair samples for DNA comparison—have been the most accurate form of population sampling on grizzly bears in the Canadian Rockies. Hopefully such methods can make inroads for increasing the accuracy of wolf and other large mammal population estimates.

Table 1: Population Estimates

Province/Territory	Estimated Wolf Population
British Columbia	7500–8000
Alberta	3500–7000
Saskatchewan	1600–5000
Manitoba	4000–6000
Ontario	8000–9000
Quebec	6000–7000
Newfoundland • Labrador • island	1000–5000* 0 (extinct since 1930)
New Brunswick	0 (extirpated since 1880)
Nova Scotia	0 (extirpated since 1900)
Prince Edward Island	0 (never present)
Nunavut	5000**
Northwest Territories	2100–5000**
Yukon	4000–4500
Total	42,700–61,500

* Labrador has not conducted any population estimates; the maximum population given is found in literature but has no validation.

* * The Northwest Territories and Nunavut have a long-estimated combined population of approximately 10,000 wolves, but this upper limit is mere speculation since no extensive population survey has ever been implemented.

Territory, Density, Pack Size and Range

Territory, density, pack size and range are different but interdependent factors of population dynamics. Territory size and movement patterns vary according to pack size, availability of prey species, physiography and seasonality. Grey wolf pack territories can vary from as small as 130 km² to as large as 13,000 km² where densities are low, such as up in the Arctic.

The average territory is 250–750 km^2. One study found that the average wolf territory size in the east slopes foothills of west-central Alberta was 640 km^2, varying between 350 and 1500 km^2, and in northeastern Alberta was 739 km^2, varying between 263 and 1071 km^2. The average winter pack size for both areas was 7 or 8 wolves (pack size increases in the spring, but not all pups survive).

Population densities of wolves also vary throughout the country. For example, in Ontario, there are three distinct areas that wolves inhabit, and wolf densities vary accordingly. Central Ontario is mainly boreal forest with low human population, and wolves here average densities of about 10 per 1000 km^2. North on the tundra, densities are much lower owing to limited and migratory prey, down to as few as 2 per 1000 km^2. In the protected area of Algonquin Provincial Park, where habitat is protected and hunting is banned, densities can be three times that of what is seen outside of the park. Both eastern wolves and grey wolves inhabit the park and prefer different prey and habitat areas, so all of the park territory is used. Eastern wolves are found throughout most of central Ontario, with Algonquin Provincial Park being the largest protected area within their range—a stronghold for the animal for conservation success to be possible. They range outside the park to the southern edge of the Canadian Shield and to Lake Nipigon in the northwest of the province; to the east they range as far as southern Quebec.

Elsewhere in Canada, wolf densities can be as low as only a few wolves per 1000 km^2, such as in northwestern British Columbia where wolf densities have been found to be about 5–11 per 1000 km^2; whereas in the coastal forests of northern Vancouver Island, densities are as high as 43 per 1000 km^2. Across the territories, there is less human impact on wolf populations and habitat, but prey densities are limited by climate and food sources in the winter or above the treeline. Wolf densities here range from 3 to 18 wolves per 1000 km^2, but with new pups in the spring, the population can reach densities as high as 100 wolves per 1000 km^2. Densities remain fairly low in Alberta, where habitat loss is significant, predator control is high and increasing industrial development prevails.

Intrinsic limitation on a wolf population in a given area is a saturation point that is reached at a certain density, based upon prey availability. The amount of prey in an area of habitat affects wolf population: rates decline as food supplies also decline. This density varies with habitat and season.

Pack sizes are not directly related to densities. Densities are determined by the number of wolves throughout an area. Pack size is the number of wolves in a pack. There may be many or just a few packs, each with many or just a few members, and the combinations over an area create varying densities. For example, Alberta has low wolf density and Ontario high; yet, according to the Alberta Sustainable Resource Development (SRD), wolf packs in Alberta have between 5 and 14 members, whereas the Ontario Ministry of Natural Resources (MNR) reports average pack sizes of between 2 and 9 wolves. Pack size varies throughout the country, although packs tend to be larger in the boreal regions. The size of a pack is not constant from year to year or from season to season. Packs tend to be larger in the winter when prey is limited, and then in the spring breeding season young pack members disperse to roam individually in search of mates to form their own packs. Pack sizes increase in late spring owing to the birth of new pups, although all pups rarely survive to winter. Pack sizes can range from a single breeding pair (and their pups in the spring) to an extended family with possibly up to 20 or more members in rare occasions, but the average pack size is 6–12 wolves (for the structure of the pack, see Reproduction, p. 59).

Wolf range depends on density. The area over which a specific pack of wolves travels is within that pack's territory. Each pack delineates and guards its territory from other wolf packs to secure breeding and hunting rights. Following prey and avoiding other wolves are the main mechanisms for establishing a pack's territory. In prey-rich areas, even a large pack won't have to traverse far at all to still have enough prey. If prey is sparse and migratory, the wolf pack will have to range farther, perhaps between different habitats, to secure the prey base and yet not trespass onto another pack's territory. For example, winter wolf ranges in BC are found in association with ungulate (hooved mammals) winter ranges. Wolves use frozen waterways as travel corridors when snow is too deep, but in the summer, they move to different altitudes and range over areas unimpeded by snow. They have less need to travel far in the spring owing to increased prey availability at that time of year: their prey base is diversified over various ecosystems.

In the arctic and subarctic where there are low prey densities, wolves often travel great distances in search of prey. Arctic wolves following migratory caribou are effectively migratory themselves, lacking territorial restrictions. They frequently must fast for days until the next successful hunt. When meat is available, they gorge themselves and sleep while digesting. However, in areas of abundant prey, wolves can eat almost daily. Helen Thayer, the first woman to walk and ski to the Magnetic North Pole, spent time in the Richardson Mountains and on some of the arctic islands, such as Pullen Island. The wolves she observed did not have to travel far to find prey and never went more than two days without feeding. These wolves would be in good condition, putting on weight that could sustain them through a cold winter with fewer prey opportunities.

Lone wolves have larger ranges but don't have territories; instead, they cross over and skirt past established pack territories. They risk encountering the wolves on whose territory they are trespassing—which can be fortuitous if it presents an opportunity for the lone wolf to find a mate or join a pack, but it can also be lethal if established wolves find the loner to be a threat. These lone wolves are typically young wolves dispersing from their families to find breeding partners, but they may also be old or ostracized and abandoned or rejected from their packs. These loners can travel hundreds of kilometres. Researchers studied three non-denning male wolves and recorded their wanderings across an area of 3077 km^2; another study estimated the average linear distance of dispersing wolves to be 90 km, ranging from 10 to 140 km. Observations by Lu Carbyn in Wood Buffalo National Park indicated ranges even larger.

TAXONOMY

Evolution

Wolves exist in Canada today after millions of years of evolution and survive after a couple hundred years of human persecution. The taxonomical record itself is continuously evolving as science finds more answers to the past. A reasonable chronology is as follows: bear in mind that this is theoretical knowledge based on fossil records, recent DNA discoveries and analyses.

The genus *Canis*, which today comprises wolves, coyotes, jackals and the domestic dog, has been widespread throughout the northern hemisphere where it originated. The first canid genus, *Hesperocyon*, appeared 37 million years ago in mid-western North America, the birthplace of all modern dogs. *Canis*, along with *Urocyon* and *Vulpes* (the two genera that foxes belong to) first made an appearance on the North American stage nine to ten million years ago.

About eight million years ago, dogs similar to small coyotes are believed to have crossed Beringia (the Bering land bridge) from North America to enter Eurasia. Various species of wolves, jackals and other canids continued to evolve in Eurasia. A subsequent rise in sea level submerged the land bridge under water, separating species from each other and resulting in evolutionary isolation.

Six million years ago, according to the existing fossil record, a wolf-like canid appeared in Western Europe, but its descendants would not travel back to North America for several million more years. Meanwhile, those ancient canids that did not wander but stayed in the Americas would evolve into different animals. *C. lepophagus* dates back four to five million years ago; its fossil remains were discovered in Texas. The numerous specimens of *C. lepophagus* that have been uncovered, interestingly, have varied proportions: this animal was small, but some individuals had delicate proportions while others had bolder, more wolf-like characteristics. Some scholars believe that *C. lepophagus* eventually evolved into *C. latrans*, the coyote.

During the Early Pleistocene (1.5–1.8 million years ago), by which time there were several forms of "wolf" in Eurasia, North American forms of the wolf line had continued to develop and diversify. *C. edwardii* is considered to be the first identifiable wolf in North America. *C. rufus* (the red wolf) appears to have descended from *C. edwardii*, but *C. lupus* did not. It was not until the Late Pleistocene (300,000 years ago) that *C. lupus* evolved in northern Eurasia and followed its cousins and migrated to North America via the Bering land bridge, south into the Yukon and Alberta. When *C. lupus* arrived in North America, it was confronted by other wolf species. *C. edwardii* and its descendants were primarily in the east, and the dire wolf (*C. dirus*) that had evolved in South America had migrated north and ranged from coast to coast as far north as southern Canada. The dire wolf was a large canid, with a massive head and tremendous teeth: the largest member of the dog family to have ever existed. The dire wolf went extinct 8000 years ago.

The grey wolf in North America is the same species as the Eurasian wolf, *C. lupus*. Today the original grey wolf species that remains in Europe is designated *C. lupus lupus*; all others are different subspecies of *C. lupus*. All members of *Canis* can interbreed and produce viable offspring, but they have been on separate evolutionary paths, and are separated taxonomically. Geneticists look at the number of haplotypes (a combination of alleles located closely together a chromosome, tending to be inherited) in DNA sequences and can see distinctions between these groups of dogs that separate them from each other.

Certain authorities recognize as many as 24 subspecies of *C. lupus* in the New World, compared to only 12 or fewer in the Old World. Of these 24 subspecies, most are or were in Canada, but several are now extinct owing to over-hunting and habitat loss. Their genetic (haplotypic) diversity has been lost. There is a growing consensus that only one or two of the subspecies designations are valid, with the others more accurately referred to as races or distinct populations, which should not be regarded as any less biologically significant.

Populations of wolves were given subspecies names in recognition of factors such as unique physical or behavioural characteristics, often owing to their habitats, or by the local people and their geo-political wildlife management jurisdictions (for example, the Manitoba wolf, *C. l. griseoalbus*). Assuming island populations were genetically isolated granted them subspecies categorization.

We appropriately call our northern wolves arctic or tundra wolves, but it is also correct to call them grey wolves. In English, all *C. lupus* is grey wolf or timber wolf (subspecies names offer alternative common names). In French the wolf is simply called loup. There are many names for wolf in native languages, such as *tuk'sit* (Algonquian), *maheegan* (Cree), *segolia* (Chipewyan), *singarti* and *amaroq* (Inuktitut dialects) and *lokwa'* (Nootka). English common names are inherently misleading—not all grey wolves are grey, not all timber wolves inhabit the forest, and so on, so we have come up with a bunch of other names. Of the lengthy list of 24 subspecies names of wolves, the following 17 are commonly thought to have lived wholly or partially in Canada. The common names repeat and overlap frequently, which is the cause of much confusion inherent in common name usage.

1. *C. l. arctos*—arctic or arctic tundra wolf
2. *C. l. beothucus*—Newfoundland wolf*
3. *C. l. bernardi*—Banks Island tundra wolf (also on Victoria Island)
4. *C. l. columbianus*—British Columbia wolf (also in the Yukon and Alberta)*
5. *C. l. crassodon*—Vancouver Island wolf
6. *C. l. griseoalbus*—Manitoba wolf or Saskatchewan timber wolf (also in Alberta)*
7. *C. l. hudsonicus*—Hudson Bay wolf or tundra wolf
8. *C. l. irremotus*—Northern Rocky Mountains wolf*
9. *C. l. labradorius*—Labrador wolf (also in northern Quebec)
10. *C. l. lycaon*—eastern timber wolf (at risk)
11. *C. l. mackenzii*—Northwest Territories wolf or Mackenzie River wolf
12. *C. l. manningi* —arctic wolf or Baffin Island wolf
13. *C. l. nubilus*—plains wolf, Great Plains wolf or buffalo wolf (also on Vancouver Island and in coastal BC)**
14. *C. l. occidentalis*—British Columbia wolf, northwest wolf, Rocky Mountain wolf or Mackenzie Valley wolf
15. *C. l. pambasileus*—northern timber wolf (in Alaska and the Yukon)
16. *C. l. tundrarum*—barren ground or arctic wolf (mainly in Alaska)
17. *C. l. youngi*—Southern Rocky Mountain wolf*

* extinct subspecies

** The original wolves of the prairies that were first considered *nubilus* are extinct. Now *nubilus* describes populations of wolves throughout most of Canada.

Subspecies of Wolves in Canada

A scientist named Nowak proposed that there are four subspecies of *C. lupus* in Canada, and most authorities today concur. The current short list is *C. l. occidentalis* (western Canada), *C. l. nubilus* (across most of Canada's forest region) and *C. l. arctos* (Arctic islands). The fourth, *C. (l.) lycaon* (southeastern Canada), is hotly debated as not being a subspecies but a separate species called *C. lycaon*.

C. l. occidentalis is commonly referred to as the timber wolf, or sometimes Rocky Mountain wolf in parts of western Canada. It lives below the treeline or in the mountains in established territories, where it preys on non-migratory prey such as moose.

C. l. nubilus was originally the name for the now-extinct wolf of the Great Plains romantically called the buffalo wolf—also known as "the loafer." This wolf was all but wiped out alongside the bison on the prairies, exterminated and deemed extinct in 1926. Bison were reintroduced and wolves moved into the prairie habitat from other populations through natural migration, throughout the boreal of the north, from the mountains of the west to the mixed wood forests of the east and up onto the tundra. They entered and took over the liberated range and name, and are now considered once again to be the Great Plains or buffalo wolf. Accordingly the species name *nubilus* was placed upon these wolves again, regardless of genetic relation to the former *nubilus*.

Nowak dealt with this subspecies name by proposing it be revised to collate most of the subspecies on that lengthy list of 17 above (such as *beothucus, crassodon, fuscus, hudsonicus, irremotus, labradorius, lycaon* (west of Michigan), *ligoni, manningi, mogollonensis, monstrabilis,* and *youngi*), and consider them all *C. l. nubilus*. So, it is with a grain of salt that we see *nubilus* become the species name for the ecotype known as the tundra wolf or caribou wolf in the territories. These wolves do not establish territories but follow migratory prey such as barren-ground caribou both above and below the treeline. We next see *nubilus* jump over the Rockies: the wolves found in coastal BC are also named *C. l. nubilus*. However, in Alaska, which shares that same coastline and is separated only by a political border, the Alexander Peninsula (the southern Pacific coastline of Alaska that should be British Columbia) deems its wolf population to be *C. l. ligoni*. Whatever these wolves are called, recent research has shown that the wolves on BC's raincoast island have 14 haplotypes whereas mainland wolves have only five. Within that list of 24 subspecies, *C. l. crassodon* was the Vancouver Island wolf. Labrador's wildlife agency still considers its wolves to be *C. l. labradorius*; perhaps it is with some sense of regional pride that regions name "their" wolves in such a manner.

C. l. arctos is probably the easiest of the subspecies to describe, mainly by geographic range. The arctic wolf inhabits the regions above the Arctic Circle, above the treeline and on the arctic islands (and in Greenland), though they do occur further south and so are not strictly an arctic species. While all arctic wolves are white, not all white wolves are arctic wolves—there are many white wolves throughout Western Canada (see more under Physiology, p. 46). The arctic wolf preys mainly on caribou, muskox and arctic hare. It is the least studied wolf population in Canada. The arctic landscape and climate prohibit any true population census or long-term observation of these white ghosts that disappear into that mysterious world of ice and snow, midnight summer sun and eternal winter darkness. The arctic wolf is somewhat smaller than its relatives of the forest. Herein lies a good example of how the dividing lines of the subspecies become more numerous. Held over from the days when that long list of 24 subspecies names was in use, many people today still consider different arctic wolf populations as distinct populations or races: *C. l. arctos* was considered to range from Melville to Ellesmere Islands; *C. l. manningi* was on Baffin Island, declared a subspecies by local wildlife authorities in 1943, and is the smallest of the arctic races; *C. l. bernardi*, the Banks Island tundra wolf, on Banks Island, but also on Victoria Island, was a white wolf with a black-tipped spine that was declared a subspecies back in 1943, about the same time it was declared extinct; farther south on the tundra of the Northwest Territories and northern Manitoba is *C. l. hudsonicus*, the Hudson Bay wolf; and in the subalpine habitat there is *C. l. mackenzii*, the Northwest Territories wolf of the Mackenzie Mountains region, also designated in 1943. To give an example of the confusion inherent in common names, the names arctic wolf or tundra wolf are often used interchangeably; however, *C. l. tundrarum*, yet another subspecies of arctic wolf, has a name that readily lends itself to the translation of tundra wolf but turns out instead to be called the barren ground wolf.

Finally, *C. (l.) lycaon* is the most controversially named wolf in Canada. Geneticists have proposed that whereas *C. lupus*

evolved in Eurasia and spread to North America, wolves in eastern North America evolved in North America; thus, *Canis lupus lycaon* should not be considered *C. lupus* at all, but *C. lycaon*—the eastern wolf that inhabits Ontario and Quebec. The eastern wolf is awaiting official designation as a separate species, although the International Union for the Conservation of Nature (IUCN) Wolf Specialist Group has not taken a position on this subject to date. Many sources already refer to it as *C. lycaon*. Rather than take a position on this and raise any hackles, I refer to the scientific name when it occurs in this book as *C. (l.) lycaon*.

Defining Populations

What defines a unique population of wolves, and what is the definition of taxonomically identifiable subspecies? Most of the proposed Canada subspecies, between a conservative few and those on more generous lists, are identified by geographic locations, morphological characteristics and behaviours that vary between groups of wolves, rather than by true genetic differences identified in the wolves' DNA. Geneticists do not dispute visible differences in morphology and behaviour but are more comfortable referring to many of these proposed subspecies of *C. lupus* as races or distinct populations. These races are distinct for occupying unique habitats within specific geographic areas; they are often considered unique for having identifiable physical characteristics, such as the arctic wolves being white. Most morphological traits are general characteristics, such as when many individuals have a specific pelage or tend to be darker or lighter, but this is a generalization rather than a firm rule, because white wolves exist among black and every pelage in between. Having a white coat does not make the wolf an arctic subspecies. Average sizes tend to vary as well. Bergmann's Rule states that animals farther north tend to be larger than their southern counterparts. Arctic wolves are an exception to this rule: the largest wolves in Canada tend to be those in the boreal forest. Significant observable variations in skull size in wolves are almost always the only morphological determinant accepted by most academics for designating non-DNA-based distinction of subspecies or race. It would be reasonable to consider these different groups of wolves as different races, which is more akin to tribal, ethnic, cultural or other anthropological categorizations in human terms.

Natural history can also, over many generations, cause a race of wolves to adapt to its environment and rely on different prey bases and hunting techniques. While these behavioural differences alone are not sufficient for designating separate subspecies, they are unique evolutionary sets of tools: one group of wolves can proficiently fish salmon on the West Coast whereas another group of wolves has the know-how to take down adult bison on the plains. Some arctic groups strategize to follow around polar bears that can provide seals as carrion, an animal a wolf could not otherwise hunt; other wolves in the arctic feed on caribou, hares, muskoxen and lemmings. Wolves are keystone players within various ecosystems, and wolves with a certain history or knowledge are very different from wolves with other natural histories. If the wolves on Vancouver Island, for example, should go extinct, they are irreplaceable in their ecosystem. No wolves from anywhere else in the world could be put in their place and function in that ecosystem in the exact same manner. They would surely survive, because wolves are intelligent and adaptable, but would have to learn by trial and error how to cope with their strange new environment, which might be a very different approach than the way the former wolves interacted with other species. Different groups of wolves may even have different immune systems to deal with the parasites, bacterium and viruses that differ between prey species and the microscopic levels of ecosystems. Wolves on the Pacific Northwest islands have learned to fish for salmon during the spawning runs; they eat only the heads, which are higher in fat and lower in parasites than the body flesh. It is an amazing evolutionary strategy that these wolves learned how to fish and how to obtain the best and avoid the worst parts of the salmon.

While most wolves are strictly territorial, some wolves have remained nomadic for generations, following the migrations of the caribou. Wolves in the boreal forest are the primary predator of all the deer species, including elk and moose. Without this natural predator, overpopulation of prey species leads to disease and habitat overgrazing, with a cascading effect throughout the food chain aptly called trophic cascades (see Predator–Prey Relationships, p. 65). Some hunters suggest that humans can take over this predator role, but wolves generally take down the weak, sick or young deer, something no human hunter is interested in.

Be they called subspecies or races, the wolf has a role in most of Canada's diverse ecology, and we want to preserve that role in its totality. For some wolves, and some areas, it's too late. Wolves have been extirpated from the Maritimes for over a century. They were never found on Prince Edward Island, and were eradicated from New Brunswick by 1880 and from Nova Scotia by 1900. The last wild wolf on the island of Newfoundland was shot in 1911 and declared officially extinct in 1930. The wolf on the island is speculated to have been a unique subspecies, as island biodiversity causes isolated evolutionary development with unique morphologies and behaviours preserved. According to accounts from early European settlers and native peoples, the wolves on the island were large and had white pelts with a black stripe down their back. The colonial government placed a bounty on that Newfoundland wolf on September 14, 1839, a reward of five pounds per animal, to make safe the livestock of the first settlers. This now-extinct subspecies is *C. l. beothucus*, or the Beothuk wolf, named after the native peoples of the island who are now also extinct. We will never see that wolf again. We do not even know what genetic information has been lost as populations of wolves have been systematically eliminated and repopulation has been diluted down with ever-reduced gene pools.

So, why does all this matter? Why not call them all grey wolves, *Canis lupus*, and be done with it? Because Canada is vast: in varied habitats and geographical niches, wolves have evolved survival strategies that ensured their success and role in their given ecosystem. A group of wolves may have an erroneous name, but it is based upon observable facts that they behave or look distinct from other groups of wolves, and recent insights into DNA analysis shows unique haplotypes in isolated populations. Diversity must be recognized and protected; wolves are not, after all, generic. And in Canada we celebrate diversity! In a book exploring Canadian wolves, there is more than just one wolf to discuss.

The Eastern Wolf and the Red Wolf

Certain species and subspecies designations are the subject of debate among taxonomists and wolf specialists, particularly the eastern wolf, *C. (l.) lycaon*. Probably better known in the conservation media over the past several years is *C. rufus*, the red wolf, not found in Canada but native to the eastern United States. The red wolf of the United States is now generally accepted as a true separate species, but while it awaits this official status it has been recognized as an endangered species for its conservation status and protection. The eastern wolf of Canada has gained the same recognition with much of the scientific community.

In the United States, the red wolf cannot be hunted. Ideally, Canada's eastern wolf would not be hunted either; however, the grey wolf and the coyote can be hunted, and most people find them difficult to differentiate between. So eastern wolves do get shot by private landowners and hunters who may or may not know what they are actually killing. Another risk factor to the eastern and red wolf populations is that their reduced numbers have resulted in a loss of pack order, and they have frequently hybridized with coyotes and domestic dogs. Red wolf biologists and conservationists are diligently trying to remove hybrids from the breeding population and back-cross each generation of pups to a more pure-bred form, but this genetic cleansing is met with some scrutiny when considering the active evolution of this subspecies may be taking advantage of benefits from hybridization. Removal of hybrids is not occurring with eastern wolves.

Eastern wolves in Canada have only recently been identified as distinct from the grey wolf, and not just related to but probably the same species as (or conspecific to) the red wolf. The Natural Resources DNA Profiling and Forensic Centre in Ontario has concluded that the eastern wolf is a distinct species of wolf very closely related to the red wolf and not a subspecies of grey wolf. There were hypotheses that red wolves were merely grey wolf–coyote hybrids that interbred during the past 12,500 years. However, recent DNA comparison of eastern wolves, grey wolves, red wolves and coyotes indicates that the eastern wolf is not a grey wolf and instead is very closely related to the far-removed population of red wolves in the southern states and more closely related to coyotes than grey wolves in Canada. Based on this evidence, perhaps 1–2 million years ago, a common ancestor of all these dogs branched apart on the evolutionary tree into two different dogs: one would stick around in North America and branch off into eastern wolves and coyotes (approximately 150,000–300,000 years ago), and the other would wander off to Eurasia and become the grey wolf before returning to North America. Eastern and red wolf ranges once connected, but in the US, the red wolf was decimated alongside the grey wolf. The few sad individuals surviving in the southeastern US are now a nation apart from their closest kin in central Ontario and southern Quebec. The eastern wolf is classified under the Ontario Fish and Wildlife Conservation Act (1997) as a Furbearing Mammal and a subspecies of *C. lupus* that will remain "protected" under the Act "until the scientific community makes a final determination on the proposal that the eastern wolf is not a *C. lupus*."

A 2007 study by Stronen further supports this theory. The researcher studied 20 haplotypes in 66 canid samples (including four coyotes) from Manitoba and Saskatchewan. Analysis of the sequence divergence of these haplotypes showed a clear separation between the grey wolf and the coyote, as well as between the grey wolf and the eastern and red wolves: the eastern and red wolves were much closer to the coyotes than to the grey wolves. Most Manitoba and all Saskatchewan wolf haplotypes grouped with other North American and European grey wolves.

Another complexity in the relationships between the grey wolf, eastern wolf and coyote in eastern Canada is the disruption of their ecology with heavy-handed extermination policies in the past. The smaller coyote occupies the open southwestern plains, whereas the larger eastern wolf inhabits the southern mixed-hardwood forest and preys upon deer, predominantly white-tailed deer. Generally, farther north in the coniferous boreal forest leading up into the taiga and tundra beyond, where there are no eastern wolves or coyotes, there are grey wolves, the large and dominant dog that the other two would avoid. Elimination of grey wolves by early settlers and in land clearing in Ontario's forests led to a northward expansion of white-tailed deer. The eastern wolves followed their prey and moved in where the grey wolves had been forced out. This is somewhat of an oversimplification, since eastern wolves also faced persecution: a settler intent on shooting any wild dog wouldn't discriminate grey wolves from eastern wolves from coyotes. But as habitats changed with the influx of settlers clearing areas for homes and agriculture, species diversity too changed. Along with the disruption of a balanced predator base, interbreeding occurred, and still occurs at the interfaces of territories. The eastern wolf suffered significant population declines and began breeding with coyotes: DNA profiles of coyotes in Ontario indicate that they have frequently hybridized with eastern and grey wolves. These hybrids are commonly referred to as brush wolves, coywolves or tweed wolves; but purebred coyotes often are given colloquial names such as brush wolf, medicine wolf, prairie wolf and little wolf, which can be misleading and confusing to the public.

The Coyote
Coyote Range

The name *coyote* is used in both English and French in Canada, though the pronunciation varies across the country from ky-OAT-ee to KY-oat to KY-oot, and these variances often cause heated debate as to which is correct and, even more importantly, which is the Canadian, not American, pronunciation. *Canis latrans* is the undisputed scientific name, which means "barking dog" in Latin. The origin of the name *coyote* comes from the Nahuatl language spoken by the Aztecs, who called the animal *coyotl*; the Spanish derivation did not pronounce the "l," dropping it as they did from many other words, such as *chocolatl*.

The coyote ranges across southern Canada, pretty much wherever there are no grey wolves. Wolves and coyotes are competitors for a similar ecological niche. Where wolves and coyotes overlap, the densities of coyotes are lower, because grey wolves are intolerant of coyotes or any other canid's presence in their territories. In the absence of wolves, coyote populations increase. This avoidance of interspecies competition is a premise of evolution, and these two species evolved to take advantage of somewhat different habitats—wolves prefer forest edges, namely boreal and montane, and primarily prey upon large ungulates, whereas coyotes prefer plains/prairies/grasslands or aspen parkland and mainly prey upon smaller animals such as rodents, lagomorphs, reptiles and birds. Coyotes are typical of the prairies, where wolves have been extirpated, but have spread north into the boreal and west along the mountain peripheries and as far east as the Maritimes. A great deal of this encroachment is parallel to urbanization of the landscape and the withdrawal of wolves from their greater range either voluntarily or by lethal force.

The evolutionary history of the coyote is separate from that of the grey wolf, which crossed the Bering land bridge back and forth during their latest evolution, but similar to the red and eastern wolves. Coyotes never left the North American continent—neither did the red wolf or eastern wolf. The eastern and red wolves look a lot more like coyotes and have frequently interbred, creating many conservation dilemmas for these endangered wolves as well as much difficulty in telling them apart from coyotes in the field.

Coyotes are frequently shot at, poisoned and trapped across their range. Many rural and suburban people see them as threats to livestock (particularly fowl and lambs) and pets (cats and small dogs). While wolves will avoid urban areas, coyotes often dwell quite close. Coyotes are easily habituated to urban environments, becoming scavengers of garbage and potentially dangerous to people. Suburban areas, with lots of scrub and brush, are full of rabbits and small rodents that coyotes prey upon. In addition, there are the abundant backyard resources of household garbage with food leftovers, as well as pet food and the small pets themselves, which are not too different from a rabbit or rodent. Some people put food out for coyotes, perhaps thinking that they are helping them, but this increased habituation can cause coyotes to lose their fear of people and become nuisance animals.

Wolf Hybrids

Wolves, coyotes and dogs are closely related, sharing a common ancestor, and are all of the same genus, *Canis*. Because all members of *Canis*—dogs, coyotes, eastern wolves, red wolves, and all the hybrids among them—can interbreed and produce fertile offspring, they are technically the same species.

Both wolves and dogs are highly social and will interbreed if the situation is suitable or necessary. That said, wolves are intolerant of any canid not part of their own family or pack. They will typically be aggressive to dogs and coyotes, as well as to wolves from other packs that breach etiquette by crossing territorial lines. This highly social pack territoriality seems to be lost in domestic dogs and even coyotes, as dogs and coyotes frequently interbreed.

Endangered eastern wolves cross-breeding with coyotes, as has been the situation with red wolves and coyotes in the US, is a concern. Hybrid eastern wolf–coyotes (coywolves or tweed wolves) have spread across the Ontario–Quebec border into New York, the New England states and the Canadian Maritime provinces (Nova Scotia, New Brunswick and Newfoundland). If pack order of eastern wolves is disrupted from over-hunting, there may be more lone wolves searching for mates. If they cannot find other wolves, coyotes may look attractive. In a natural system, wolves and coyotes avoid each other as competitors. Coywolves or tweed wolves are smaller than wolves, but with a larger stature, larger skull and larger stronger jaws than coyotes. They still hunt rodents as coyotes do, but have demonstrated the capacity to take down deer. They also retain the temperament to tolerate close coexistence with humans, which presents an undesirable potential for habituation, but from a species perspective, this is an advantage over wolves, which avoid human settlement.

Interbreeding between coyotes and grey wolves was undocumented until recent years. Coyotes and grey wolves both have stable populations in Canada and follow their natural behavioural instincts to stick to their own species. Wolves and coyotes avoid each other and rarely overlap in their territories. Lu Carbyn, who studied wolves in the delta of Wood Buffalo National Park for over 16 years, only saw a coyote in the delta once. However, after heavy wolf culling campaigns, coyotes were reportedly common in the delta. Typically, lone grey wolves, if of healthy breeding age, are males kicked out of their mother's pack and sent out to form packs of their own. If wolf populations are low, established packs remain small and do not get divided up to allow for new males to establish new packs. The lone males may more likely find female coyotes as willing mates.

Dog–wolf hybrids are sometimes less wolf and more junk-yard dog, hanging out at garbage dumps and scavenging meals of food scraps from local households. Feral dog–wolf hybrids (typically offspring of a domestic dog female and wolf male, left to run feral) have long been considered more aggressive and dysfunctional than wild wolves and are often the animals responsible for attacks on people's dogs. Often it is not known what individual animals caused damage or injury, and this can lead to manhunts on innocent animals.

Dogs are often considered a subspecies of wolf, *C. l. familiaris*, rather than *C. familiaris*; in other words, not a truly evolved species on their own but domesticated long ago from wild wolf ancestors. It is interesting to consider that the common dog is a subspecies of a species protected in most of its international range as endangered. Though hybridization between dogs and wolves has been perceived to be frequent throughout the centuries, dogs and grey wolves do not interbreed often in the wild when wolf pack social status is strong and healthy. A dog would rarely have the strength to usurp a wolf of its breeding status within its pack and would likely get itself killed; stray dogs and lone wolves looking to establish a pack may have a more likely chance for romance, especially if the female is the dog and the male is the wolf. Small "yappy" dogs are more likely to become a snack than a mate for a wolf.

Dogs and grey wolves interbreeding more often occurs through deliberate breeding by humans trying to obtain the desired qualities of both species in one animal. The qualities in wolves that people want to breed into the domestic dog are strength, stamina and instincts, as well as the thick luxurious coats that we admire in wolves; trying to retain the loyalty of the domestic dog in combination with these attributes has resulted in the wolf–dog hybrid. However, most often dogs are selected for cross-breeding for their breed's aggressive traits, for guarding or hunting. The result is an offspring with far less control over its aggressive instincts than wolves have. The hybrid will often attack and fight to kill any animal it encounters, whereas wolves only kill what they intend to eat (no wolves are known to surplus kill) and will avoid danger whenever possible. Killing between wolves occurs when rival dominant males vie for breeding rights. Usually the weaker will retreat if defeat is imminent, although it is not unusual for it to die trying.

Lois Crisler raised wolves in Alaska in the 1950s and documented the contrasting behaviour of her wolf–dog hybrids to that of the purebred wolves and dogs. The hybrids displayed what Crisler called an "inbred schizophrenia," with conflicting wild and tame personalities. Crisler felt that these conflicting natures caused the animals to display emotions alternating between rage and anxiety. Many owners of wolf–dog hybrids agree that these animals cannot be treated as dogs and that too often the animals end up permanently chained or caged. Hybrids perceive their highly social wolf nature, making them long for the freedom to roam, hunt and join a pack. Owners that cannot find a way to pacify this longing end up with animals that are forced to obey human rules, accept confinement and live a life of, as Crisler put it, "submission and torment." Many of these animals have attacked dogs and domestic animals either in aggression or in hunger. Some owners who no longer want or no longer can deal with these unhappy animals have released them, but sadly, these hybrids don't have the survival skills to be granted their freedom. Many hybrids are euthanized.

Physiology

Grey Wolves

A highly evolved hunter and survivor, the wolf is admired for its speed and strength. It is a pursuit predator with stamina and endurance, enabling it to run for several kilometres in the chase. It will not pursue prey over long distances but has success with an ambush style, getting close to the prey before making an attack. The wolf's long hind legs allow average top running speeds of 40–55 km per hour over a few kilometres, but much faster in short bursts. The wolf can cover large distances in search of prey: radio-collared wolves are frequently recorded covering averages of 30–65 km in a day, with extreme traverses of up to 120 km a day where prey is scarce. In areas such as the Northwest Territories, these travels occur over difficult mountainous or frozen winter terrain.

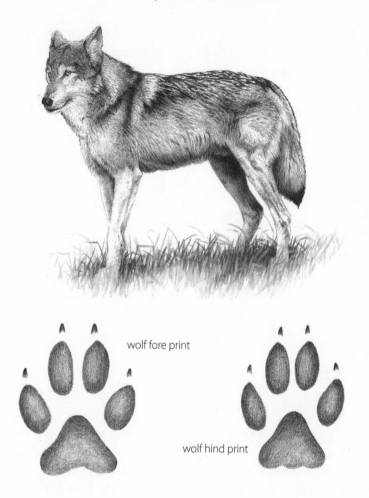

wolf fore print

wolf hind print

The wolf's stride is about 57 cm; walking, a wolf's stride is 38–80 cm, running, around 90 cm. Mech reported a wolf bounding over 5 m in pursuit of a moose. Wolf tracks fall in a straight line, the hind feet stepping into the tracks of the forefeet for easier passage in deep snow, which is challenging for individual wolves. A pack travels single file, with the leader breaking trail and the followers stepping in the leader's tracks. Once the leader tires, a new member of the pack takes the lead, much the same way as a flock of geese fly in formation and change lead position as an energy-saving strategy. The fore print is 10–14 cm long and 6.5–13 cm wide, and the hind print is slightly smaller. The wolf's feet are large, possibly as much as twice the surface area of a dog of the same stature, and well padded. Hence the Russian proverb that finds its place in nearly every book on wolves, "a wolf is kept fed by its feet."

wolf walking trail

wolf trotting trail

Wolves vary in weight and height across the country, but adult males are larger than adult females. Grey wolves, including arctic wolves, stand about 60–90 cm to the shoulder with body lengths of 135–200 cm from the tip of the nose to the tip of the tail (tails are nearly a quarter of the total body length). Robustness varies with population and is probably to some degree related to food source and availability. Wolves of northwestern and western Canada are larger than those of southeastern Canada and the Arctic. Alberta wolves are large relative to other wolves on the same latitude—about 40–45% heavier on average than wolves of the Great Lakes region. The largest trophy wolves recorded, with the greatest skull lengths and widths, have been taken from Alberta and British Columbia. The heaviest wolf on record in Canada was shot in Jasper National Park by a park warden in 1945; that wolf weighed 78 kg (though there is some question among biologists about this record). Wolves on the arctic islands tend to be slight of build; the climate is harsher and prey is less abundant. Arctic wolf females weigh 25–32 kg, and males weigh up to 36 kg. Grey wolves in the rest of Canada have much more variability, with weights of 30–40 kg in females and records of over 60 kg in males (though the average range is 35–50 kg).

Carbyn's data from captured wolves in Wood Buffalo National Park from 1978 to 1981 recorded the heaviest male at 58 kg, the heaviest female at 41 kg, the average adult male at 47 kg and the average adult female at 39 kg. Pups, captured in midwinter, weighed an average of 33 kg.

The wolf's jaws of 42 teeth boast a crushing power of 105.46 kilogram-force per square centimetre. The distance between the canines, the wolf's fangs, is around 4 cm.

In general, predators' eyes—including humans'—are set in the front of the face. A forward-directing gaze sets the predator's visual field to target ahead on its prey. Perhaps this affinity furthers our sense of kinship with the wolf. Wolves' eyes glow in the dark as light reflects off the tapetum lucidum layer of the eye, which is suspected to improve night vision. Wolves are born with blind infant-blue eyes, which turn to shades of amber, brown or green.

A wolf's coat, which is thickest in the winter, has an insulating under-fur and a coarse outer layer of long guard hairs (up to 10 cm long). Wolves can be a variety of colours from pure white to jet black, with shades of grey, brown and cream. A typical Great Plains wolf may have a coat of grey, black or buff with reddish colouring. The colour variation Carbyn observed in Wood Buffalo's wolves appeared to have three phases (seen from a distance): grey, white or black. The subtleties Carbyn observed were black, grey black, white, yellow white, blonde, brownish grey, grey grizzled, brownish black and grey brown with black streaks. He never saw a blue-black wolf in his study area in Wood Buffalo National Park, but did see this colour phase in Jasper National Park, in the Mackenzie Bison

Sanctuary and the Hay Camp area within Wood Buffalo National Park. He describes the blue-black colour as the pelage of an elderly black wolf, which tends to turn white with age, going through a blue phase. Most of Carbyn's study wolves were grey, but half as many were white or black. White wolves were more common in the delta than in the southern regions of the park. Carbyn attributed this difference to proximity to tundra regions and that caribou wolves may have moved south to breed with the Wood Buffalo wolves.

Rocky Mountain wolves have coats of grey, black, white, tan and even bluish, with grey or black being the most common. West Coast wolves are often black while the wolves on the Pacific Northwest islands have a unique ochre colour.

Arctic wolves are white or cream-coloured. This is characteristic of arctic species such as polar bears, arctic foxes, arctic hares, and so on. Some arctic species are only white in the winter for camouflage, but white fur has other functions in arctic winter—white hair shafts have more air pockets than pigmented hair shafts. These air pockets function like insulation, trapping warm air near to the skin. This characteristic is advantageous in cold winter climates.

As would be expected, wolf scat is similar in shape to that of a large dog. You can recognize the scat of a wolf from that of a dog because wolf scat typically has fur and bones in it from the wolves' prey. Old scat will turn white.

Eastern Wolves

Eastern wolves (*C. (l) lycaon*) are smaller than grey wolves and often confused with coyotes. The eastern wolf stands about the same height as a grey wolf but tends not to be as long and nor as hefty: height 60–68 cm, length 1–2 m (males average 164 cm, females 155 cm), weight 23–36 kg (males average 30 kg, females 24 kg). They have not been observed with the black or white pelage but instead have reddish brown points (muzzle, behind the ears and lower legs) on a black, white and grey–mottled overall pelage.

Wolves in Algonquin Provincial Park are almost certainly eastern wolves; coyotes are mostly absent from the park since they are outcompeted for territory by wolves (wolves will kill coyotes caught in their territories) and coyotes are less associated with forested habitats. This is not to say that these overlaps have not occurred. There is evidence of eastern wolf–coyote hybrids in the park, but these hybrids are believed to be rare and occur at the park borders. Greater rates of hybridization in the past are associated with the extensive land clearing common in the 1800s and early 1900s.

Eastern wolves are protected within Algonquin Provincial Park and the surrounding townships, but members of the protected population risk being shot when they venture beyond this area, particularly when they hunt white-tailed deer. Coyotes are also protected in the park and surrounding townships, because eastern wolves are frequently misidentified as coyotes and shot. A pack of eastern wolves may have a territory up to 500 km² but the average is about 150 km². While the government of Ontario recognizes the eastern wolf as an endangered species, it is technically still considered *C. lupus* and therefore not officially protected in Canada. Surveys show that over 90% of Ontarians support protection of the eastern wolf as a species at risk.

Comparison with Coyotes

The closest relative of the wolf in Canada is the coyote. It is closely related in morphology, behaviour and natural history. While the difference between a coyote and a grey wolf is fairly obvious, it is not so easy to distinguish a coyote from an eastern wolf; this similarity has been a management problem for protecting the endangered eastern wolf from being shot, trapped or poisoned by people believing that they are killing coyotes (coyotes have little to no protection in most of the country).

Several key differences help to identify a coyote from a wolf. One important distinguishing feature is size. The coyote weighs 9–23 kg, a fraction of the mass of an adult male grey wolf, but large male coyotes are pretty close in size to the

Coyote

diminutive frame of the eastern wolf. Under its thick fur, the coyote has a slight frame. The body length of an adult coyote is 1.2–1.5 m, which includes the bushy 30–40 cm-long tail, and height is 58–66 cm at the shoulder. The female is on the lower end of these measurement ranges, being usually four-fifths as large as the male.

coyote galloping

Coyote pelage is generally a tawny grey with black-tipped guard hair on the hind part of the back and tail, which also has a black tip. The legs, paws, muzzle and back of the ears are more yellowish in colour; the throat, belly and insides of the ears are pale. Overall, this mottled grey pelage is very similar in all three species—the grey and eastern wolves and the coyote—especially when seen at a distance.

BEHAVIOUR

Communication

Unique moments like this
are special somehow,
for places are dwindling
where Timber Wolves howl.
Their voice bespeaks wildness.
It has then; it must now.

–J. Butler, "The Howl," *Dialog with a Frog on a Log*

The wolf is the ancestor of all domestic dogs and was the first domesticated animal 10,000–12,000 years ago in the Middle East. Man's best friend today, however, is considered a less intelligent animal—apologies to all you dog owners! Though surely your dog is the exception to the rule, dogs generally demonstrate the effects of centuries of domestication and generations of inbreeding—and the more selectively bred the dog, the less intelligent, as any owner of a mutt will agree! However, the same qualities loved in dogs can be seen in wolves, which make the years of human persecution of wolves tragically ironic. Most dog owners will tell of the dog's vastly expressive face, loyalty, trust and keen sensitivity to emotions. Therefore, it should not be surprising to hear of the same features in wolves, from which the dog was bred. Emotions ranging from protective and aggressive hostility to loving affection can be seen in the communication skills of wolves.

Wolves are considered highly intelligent by comparative studies of other mammals. This conclusion is partially based upon the size of the brain but also upon their ability to learn from mistakes and modify behaviours based upon outcomes of previous experiences; furthermore, they are able to pass along this learned behaviour to their young. Young wolves learn how to find food sources and how to avoid danger. They have highly intricate communication and social skills. They adapt hunting strategies according to learned cause-and-effect outcomes.

Wolves communicate in three ways: vocalization, scent and visual signal. Indeed, they have keen senses of hearing, smell and vision.

The vocalizations of the wolf are diverse: they growl and snarl to show aggression, bark as an alarm signal (they don't obsessively bark and yap like domestic dogs) and make a sort of squeak to call the pups. But the most iconic the wolf's vocal repertoire, and of all other voices of the Canadian wilderness except perhaps the loon, is the wolf's howl.

Pragmatically, the howl serves to communicate with and locate other pack members, or other packs. The wolf's howl helps wolves convey information to other wolves over great distances to establish pack territories, reunites separated pack members and maintains separation from members of other packs, and surely a whole lot more. It creates pack cohesion and bonding as the entire pack howls in harmony, each wolf with its own resonance, tenor and pitch. But the howl of the wolf is undoubtedly also an expression of emotion. Hearing the call of the wolf is an experience reputed beyond beauty, touching the listener deeply with its emotion.

Few people are unmoved by hearing a wolf howl, for it indeed conveys something deeper than a simple communication of location. Wolves howl excitedly in anticipation of the hunt and after that hunt's success. They howl with similar excitement when pups are born, and there is an audible change to a slow, mournful howl when a pack member dies. It is hard to dispute that wolves howl in celebration, in joy and, indeed, in mourning. And it seems that wolves howl for the pure pleasure of howling. They are singing their songs, telling their stories. Though many people will leap at the following statement as shamelessly anthropomorphic, the howl is a part of wolf culture. I do not find it awkward to consider that many animals, just like humans, share knowledge, stories, wisdom and perhaps even artistry when they sing. When wolves, whales or birds sing, they pass their songs through the generations like an oral history. Perhaps howling, or singing, is similar to our human rituals of song, dance and music—often for beauty's sake alone, perhaps for connection with some mysterious divinity, perhaps for expression of the soul. It is fun to ponder the possibilities and mysteries that science cannot explain.

With less romantic connotations—though undeniably important in the sex lives of wolves—scent conveys important messages. Endorphins and other chemical messages are important forms of wolf communication, particularly during breeding season, though they are still little understood by humans (even though we too use them without even realizing!). Wolves also disperse these messages of scent by urinating over strategic locations. Most often the only wolves that scent-mark to affirm their breeding status are the breeding pair; a subordinate wolf would be challenging the breeding wolf by scent-marking. Wolves scent-mark around property, such as food caches, prey carcasses and dens. Their sense of smell allows them to detect prey over significant distances, as well as to detect danger, including humans. They mark large territories to establish hunting zones to partition prey from other wolf packs and keep out non-pack members. Wolves urinate to mark their territory to notify other wolves not to trespass; wolves can clearly recognize boundaries made by other wolves in this fashion.

Studying wolves in Alberta, Carbyn observed two adult wolves from one pack (the "Fly Camp" pack) engaging with another pack (the "Lousy Creek" pack) and theorized that "some individuals can readily go back and forth between packs and be accepted in both." This finding raises another question, posed by Carbyn: which pack would these two individuals be loyal to if the two packs clashed? Likely the two packs are subunits of a larger pack, or the wolves are related to each other by two females in a pack having produced litters, and would not clash. Biologist Doug Smith also observed interbreeding between packs in Yellowstone National Park, as well as more than one male or female in a pack breeding. The high density of wolves in close proximity to each other and the abundant food availability are believed to contribute to these situations.

The wolf's physical language is best seen in the relationships wolves have with each other. The wolf's mouth is expressive; there are obvious messages conveyed by a snarl with a curled lip, by bared teeth and a wrinkled nose or by the tongue lagging open-mouthed with a happy face. There is even a well-documented identification of the wolf smile. Play fighting with jaws around faces and throats is different than closed-eye nuzzles of affection. Simple gestures with complex messages are part of wolf vocabulary and dialogue. Wolves' eyes are extremely expressive. A direct stare is threatening, and usually the receiving wolf diverts its own gaze to show submission or friendly intention. A wide, innocent gaze is playful. The pupils change their dilation quickly with changes of emotion. Wolf eyesight is acute and penetrating. A human making eye contact with a wolf is rare, in the wild or captivity, unless the wolf's intention is to threaten or to play. The wolf will otherwise divert its eyes, in an elusiveness or coyness that seems to keep the wolf's world shrouded from us in mystery. Eye contact is an intimate, deeply meaningful communication.

There is a social order within the family. The breeding pair stands tall with their tails held high. The other adults hold their tails down and keep their bodies lower when approaching the breeding pair. The breeding male is often the largest and strongest of the group. All other members of the pack are subordinate and submissive in body language and feeding privileges, including the breeding female, who is next in line for this display of respect from the rest of the pack.

Submission is an important message a wolf must clearly convey, and wolf researchers have identified two modes of submission: active and passive. Food begging, for example, is a form of active submission. This is expressed by tail wagging, ear lowering and licking—Mech describes this last gesture as "licking up," much like the term "kissing up," which is a pretty apt description. The submissive wolf does not actually lick the other wolf, but laps its tongue much like Pavlov's dog might as he licks his chops in anticipation of his dinner. At this request, the other wolf might regurgitate food to the submissive wolf, likely a pup or another wolf that was unable to join the successful hunt. Biologists have observed the gifting of food from subordinates to the breeding male wolf. Conversely, subordinates, usually young or infirm not joining the hunt, beg for a regurgitated meal from higher-ranking wolves. The breeding male gifts food to his mate or allows her to snatch it from him, and she then regurgitates meals to his pups. Food sharing appears to instil good relations between members of the pack. A wolf rolling onto its side or back before a dominant wolf demonstrates passive submission. Mech described this submission as common in the Ellesmere Island wolves he studied. In passive submission, the passive wolf makes itself as vulnerable as possible, exposing its soft underbelly and groin and allowing the dominant wolf to sniff at its groin or genitals.

The pack is a tight group, raising young, hunting and playing together. Conflicts only arise, if ever, if an individual is simply out of line, in the way or in some way disrespecting the other members of the pack by not knowing its place in the pecking order or the subtle social and even moral codes of the pack. Not adhering to these rules can get a wolf physically attacked, ostracized from the pack or killed.

Reproduction

Wolves have a fairly wide range of age for reaching sexual maturity, from about 22 months to four years old, but on average reach sexual maturity in their third year. Breeding time varies with latitude (farther north, it takes place later) but occurs between January and April. An established pack will have one breeding pair, but this is not a hard-and-fast rule. A pack often starts out as a breeding pair, with their pups forming the pack. At subsequent generations pups may leave to start packs of their own or they may stay and breed within the pack. It is a flexible and dynamic unit that scientists are still observing and documenting.

After a nine-week (63-day) gestation, the female wolf excavates a birthing den, typically into the side of a hill or embankment. Sometimes she enlarges an existing burrow made by a fox

or other burrowing mammal, or uses a large hollow tree stump or log. Most often the maternity den is reused year after year by the same pack. It is usually near a water source that the female can easily and discreetly access. The burrow opening is generally 50–65 cm wide with a mound of excavated sand or soil at the entrance. The den extends back 2–10 m.

Five to seven pups (as few as two or three, or more than eight, are possible) are born in late May to early June. Litters are smaller in the far north than in the south, likely owing to availability and density of prey. Newborn pups weigh about 450 g. Born blind, their blue eyes open at 9–15 days, and within a week of opening their eyes, they are strong enough to start standing or walking. At two to three weeks of age, the pups start to explore the exit of the den, and their world begins to expand. Members of the pack bring the mother wolf meat—either fresh or regurgitated—because the mother wolf stays with the newborn pups and does not join the hunt until the pups are older.

About a month after the pups are born, the mother wolf moves them from the whelping den to a series of larger summer rendezvous sites excavated in banks or shallow hillsides, among the roots of large trees, in hollow logs or in rock crevices. Pups are moved to these rendezvous sites periodically as they grow, moving farther from the maternity den and closer to the pack. These dens may have several entrances 30–60 cm wide, and the tunnel is about 1–5 m long. Pups are fed regurgitated food for about 45 days until they can start to tear into meat brought back by the other members of the pack. They are weaned at six to eight weeks of age and as they get older, the mother wolf may occasionally leave the pups alone or in the care of a babysitter—another member of the pack, perhaps a teenager or elder wolf that does not join the hunt. They may be left for a day, or rarely for a couple of days or longer. It is important that the rendezvous sites have ample cover, so the pups can loaf about and play without detection from predators, and are near water for drinking.

The pups are raised by the entire pack. By mid-autumn, at a few months of age, they are learning how to hunt. Pups will start to chase and kill small quarry of their own, such as mice and butterflies. By about four months of age, pups join the pack on an actual hunt, travelling far from the den, learning the strategies of the hunt and helping take down large game. A pup reaches adult size in its first year. On average, according to numerous studies, less than half of pups survive to maturity.

Eventually, as early as one year of age and typically by three years of age, most pups leave to join other packs or find mates and form packs of their own. Some pups may stay with the mother's pack, becoming the next breeders, or simply replace pack members who die.

When a pup leaves its pack to enter into another established pack, it is somewhat akin to marrying into a family. Naturally, allowing unrelated wolves into a family for breeding purposes keeps genetic diversity.

If a pack becomes larger than average, there may be more than one breeding pair if prey availability is abundant. Most likely there would be a second, even possibly a third, breeding female with the same breeding male, rather than two independent breeding pairs. In a truly communal approach to raising the young, other females are able to nurse the pups as a result of pseudopregnancy. Pseudopregnancy, a false pregnancy, is a little-understood phenomenon in wolves: non-pregnant female wolves will lactate and be "wet nurses" to another female's pups. Body chemistry is believed to be behind this strange phenomenon. The word *phenomenon* just indicates that we simply don't understand how something works—there is a scientific explanation, but we haven't figured it out yet. There are many such phenomena in the animal kingdom.

The average wolf pack consists of about six to nine wolves, though size ranges widely in different areas of Canada (see Territory, Density, Pack Size and Range, p. 23). This number includes the pups of the year, and all members are typically related. In other words, a pack is more or less a family: a breeding pair, sometimes a sibling, aunt or uncle of another member of the pack, elder post-reproductive individuals, a few offspring—two-year-olds, yearlings and new pups of the year. The eldest wolf may not necessarily be one of the breeding pair, but will usually still merit respect from the other pack members as an elder. Most packs also consist of adults who never sought after breeding partners inside or outside the pack, but who may become breeders if the current breeder dies. There tends to be more female family members in the pack than males—to reproduce within the pack if opportunity arises—with unrelated individuals entering from other families. If one or both members of the current breeding pair cease breeding, the opportunity will arise for a new member of the pack to accept this responsibility. Typically, but not necessarily, the breeding female is a pack member and the breeding male enters from another pack. This is why most male pups disperse from the pack whereas female pups remain with the family, making it somewhat of a matriarchy.

The term "alpha pair" is not necessarily accurate in wolf breeding hierarchy; rather, they are the *breeding* pair. They may not be the leaders in other social hierarchies in the pack; for example, a non-breeding individual may be a leader in the hunt. Mech proposes dismantling the alpha categorization, insisting it is outdated. He describes the alpha/breeding pair: "I conclude that the typical wolf pack is a family, with the adult parents guiding the activities of the group in a division-of-labor system in which the female predominates primarily in such activities as pup care and defense and the male primarily in foraging and food-provisioning and the travels associated with them."

Barry Lopez interviewed researchers about wolf–human relations between the arctic wolves of Alaska and the Nunamiut peoples (and then wrote *Of Wolves and Men* in 1978) and also dismisses the alpha theory. "Much has been made of the 'hierarchical' structure of wolf packs, but... notions about rigid rankings, harsh discipline, and alpha male leadership owe more to human than to wolf culture. Wolf social organization is more dynamic, responsive to individual personalities and circumstances. Roles may change, over time and depending on the business at hand."

Mech furthers that "alpha" should be reserved for the rare cases of large packs with multiple litters of pups where one pair, likely the older breeders, is dominant over the younger breeders. Dominance at feeding at the kill or leading the direction of the pack's travels are stronger indicators of dominance than whether or not a wolf is a breeder in the pack. The genetic relationships between the females in the pack are unknown but suspected to be a matriarch and one or more daughters. The relationship of the breeding male(s), who may be a patriarch and unrelated adoptees, to the females is also little understood.

The lifespan of a wolf in the wild can be in the early teens, but the average is only about five or six years. The oldest captive wolves on record reached 17 and 18 years of age. In the wild, lifespan is significantly truncated by fatal accidents, disease, fights with other wolves or other large predators or, more commonly, human involvement (trapping, shooting, poisoning).

When pack structure is disrupted, as is the case when wolf culling occurs, a once-large pack may result in several small packs. When wolf density is reduced, the wolf population typically recovers within one or two seasons. For this reason, most biologists concur that unless wolf culling is actively maintained in perpetuity, it is biologically ineffective. A policy of continuous, deliberate culling of wolves is not only costly from a management perspective, but there is also evidence that the ecosystem's overall health is terribly compromised.

Predation/Hunting Strategy

Each pack lives and hunts in an exclusive territory that is clearly defined and communicated to other wolf packs and lone wolves, mainly through scent-marking and howling. Aggressive encounters with other packs may occur but further emphasize and maintain territorial boundaries.

Typically one wolf will direct the hunt, leading the pack to the location of the prey and orchestrating the attack. Body language is subtle and refined, beyond our human vocabulary of understanding. Each member of the hunting party knows its role, and the synchronicity seems choreographed. The prey target is identified for a particular vulnerability: isolation from the herd by a physical barrier or perhaps simply absent-mindedness, weakness from an injury or illness or, in the spring, being young and unguarded. Wolves will chase a herd to try to isolate an individual. Not every attempt at bringing down prey is successful. Wolves will also feed on the carrion of large animals that have died of natural causes.

If the wolves can maintain the prey's disadvantage, sometimes by running the prey to exhaustion, the kill comes by taking the animal down by severing leg muscles and seizing the flanks and usually also the head and throat. The downed animal is then disembowelled. It is vicious and brutal to

observe, and surely this kill style has had a role in giving the wolf its nasty reputation in folklore and fairy tales (and even to squeamish viewers of *National Geographic* documentaries).

Once the prey is down, the pack will feed for a day or two. If there are members of the pack left behind at a den (pups, nursing females, elders unable to hunt, young wolves not yet joining the hunt), part of the prey will be carried back. The gorged hunters may also regurgitate some of the undigested meal carried in their stomachs.

PREDATOR–PREY RELATIONSHIPS

Where wolves have become established, their presence in the ecological community has increased biodiversity and enhanced ecosystem integrity. Depredations to livestock have been lower than expected and economic benefits from tourism have been positive.

–North American Section of the Society
for Conservation Biology

Top-down vs. Bottom-up Ecology

In ecological terms, we know wolves play an important role in nature. Long-term studies in Algonquin Provincial Park in Canada and Yellowstone National Park and Isle Royale National Park in the United States have illustrated the complex interactions between wolves and other species of plants and animals (both prey species and other predators and scavengers). In ecosystems where wolves have been removed, there is further evidence that wolves affect much more than just their prey. One study found that where wolves had been long absent, there was an indirect result of decreased aspen and willow owing to overgrazing by increased ungulates, which in effect reduced the songbird species' diversity and abundance.

With their smaller numbers, the influence of top predators on an ecosystem was previously believed to be negligible compared to the amount of solar energy plants obtain to directly feed herbivores and thus determine animal populations. By what is called bottom-up ecology, the plant kingdom is the biomass that dictates the abundance of herbivores, leaving predators ultimately at the mercy of the health of the system below. The 10% rule of bottom-up ecology states that top predators would be 10% of the population of herbivores, which would be 10% of plant biomass. However, there is a counter-scenario to bottom-up ecology.

It takes a long time—years and years—to see the impact large predators can have on systems. However, other predators, such as marine invertebrates, have short life cycles. One now-famous study by biologist Robert Pain gave a very clear example of how predators have a very important influence on a system. Pain's research showed an alternative scenario to bottom-up ecology, and involved a specific starfish (*Pisator ocraceus*), which is a top predator in a tide pool. In this predator's absence from the sample plots, overall diversity of the tide pool actually declined rather than increased. The reason was that the starfish preyed mostly on a species of mussel (*Mytilus californianus*), which in the absence of its predator outcompeted other species for available space on the rocks. The starfish may occasionally prey upon these other species as well, but when the starfish kept the pushy mussel in check, the other species had space in the tide pool. This realization was coined top-down ecology and proved that top predators do indeed influence the biodiversity of an ecosystem, and are not merely the last tiles to fall in a chain of dominoes.

For decades, wolves were studied on Isle Royale, Michigan, where island ecology creates an almost closed system, preventing migration of terrestrial species in or out. Before wolves were introduced, moose were overly abundant and their only controlling factors were disease or starvation. High moose numbers had a negative impact on vegetation, which in turn negatively impacted health and viability in populations of other herbivores, birds and smaller predators. The whole system was out of balance. After wolves were introduced, balance slowly began to be achieved. Populations of wolves and moose are dynamic, rising and falling in relation to each other in a balanced equilibrium, debunking the management myth that wolves have to be controlled by human intervention to prevent them from decimating game populations.

Another example is in Yellowstone National Park in Wyoming. When wolves were removed from the park so that it would be more suitable for human recreation, the wolves' prey species overpopulated, causing overgrazing and starvation, negatively impacting plants and the other animals that rely upon them, and also making room for other predators such as foxes, coyotes, weasels and even feral dogs and cats. These animals increased the predation of songbirds and amphibians. In parts of Canada and the US where wolves were removed, coyotes moved into the vacated niche and have become an even worse problem in human–wildlife conflict since coyotes are easily habituated to urban settings. To this day Banff National Park has problems with over-abundant elk in and around the townsite that causes complaints from residents and sometimes dangerous situations for tourists, as well

as overgrazing. The elk have become habituated and overpopulated since the 1960s, when Banff deliberately removed wolves from the park for much the same reasons Yellowstone did. Wolves are back now, but cut off from their prey by roads, rails, ski trails and urban development, and the predator–prey imbalance persists as a major wildlife management concern. Wolves cannot control the elk overpopulation if they cannot get to the elk. Wolves have had to change their prey focus, sometimes to more status-vulnerable species, leading to many other ecological problems.

Time and time again, in a system void of its formerly occurring wolf population, the primary ungulate prey species increases in population and thus in density. As this herbivore density increases, vegetation becomes overgrazed and herbivores begin competing against each other for food and space. One species that is a generalist may outcompete others that are more specialized. While hunters may be happy to see an increase in elk, there may be a coinciding decrease in moose, or there could be an increase in deer coinciding with a decrease in caribou. Wolf culls are theoretically supposed to increase game opportunities for hunters and help sensitive species such as woodland caribou, but sensitive species also typically decline through the influx of other ungulates into a habitat liberated of wolves. The caribou simply has one pressure (predators) replaced by another pressure (competitive herbivores).

While nobody may be noticing, a loss of wolves may also result in declines of beavers (which affects wetlands) or declines in songbirds, wildflowers and pollinating insects as a result of overgrazing by prey species. Overall biodiversity declines. But there will be a lot of elk or deer, and hunters can happily shoot at them and consider them a managed population.

Removal of wolves sometimes causes the populations of other predators, such as coyotes, bears or cougars, to increase, which has an affect on prey species. Possibly, a species that did not have to contend with these predators before will have to modify its survival strategies in a very fast behavioural evolution. Once humans realize that wolves need to be put back into the system, or allowed to repopulate, the scene and prey population dynamics meanwhile may have changed. When the wolf population is in recovery, wolves may hunt alternative prey than what was their primary prey before the cull. Ungulates that suffered from competition from elk or deer will now be preyed upon by wolves. These ungulates may have become more vulnerable than before the wolves were removed.

The overgrazing from the increased population of generalist species may cause changes to vegetation composition. By contrast, declines in species such as elk may also bring about slow changes to the plant community, such as increased aspen and willow: first succession forest species that can increase biodiversity in cleared areas but change a grassland to a forest, or change water distribution and abundance and hold river banks from erosion.

Wolf predation can keep ungulate levels low if populations have already declined as a result of other limiting factors such as severe winters. Hunting has an additional impact on ungulate populations. Most hunters will consent to a reduced quota but rarely to a moratorium on hunting, and most always with resentment if wolves are not culled as well. It's as if hunters, considering themselves as having equal rights to the wolves, feel that if they can't have venison for dinner then why should the wolves—apparently not realizing that wolves don't have Costco as a backup.

Hunters may consider themselves a suitable substitute for predators or wolves, by keeping species such as deer or elk in check in a human hunting strategy. But the inferior individuals are not hunted. Few hunters want to take home a sickly looking deer for dinner or to hang on their wall. Instead, the biggest, strongest and healthiest are the targets, effectively taking them out of the gene pool and putting them on the hunters' walls or plates. In a Darwinian sense, those impressive bucks have the strength of mind and body the species needs to survive. The natural system did not evolve with men on Ski-doos or in airplanes with high-powered scopes and rifles taking down the species' greatest investments. Humans take the biggest and best, leaving a weaker gene pool and fewer bulls to defend calves (increasing predation rates on calves is an added negative impact of human hunting styles). But wolves most often take (in addition to undefended young) the sick, slow and perhaps less intelligent, leaving the smarter and stronger members of the herd to reproduce. In Wood Buffalo National Park, where bison with tuberculosis have been a problem in the past, Bill Fuller of the Canadian Wildlife Service considered that wolves taking down sick bison with advanced TB sanitized the herd. In the early 1980s, moose populations in northwestern Alberta faced an epidemic of severe tick infestations. Wolves took advantage of the abundant supply of easy-to-hunt, weak moose. Removing the severely infected moose reduced the spread of ticks to uninfected moose; the moose population was significantly decreased but was able to rebound with the healthy stock that survived.

In a system where wolves are ecologically effective, diversity increases and predation on threatened ungulate populations decreases. Overall game species populations are healthy, permitting a reasonable human harvest, and livestock depredation also lessens owing to increased natural prey abundance.

However, ecological effectiveness typically requires a much larger wolf population than many jurisdictions are comfortable with. In the United States, the wolf may be delisted from the endangered species list simply because its minimum viable population has been achieved after 60 years of absence. A reintroduction program seeking ecological integrity and long-term sustainability cannot work with minimums.

Prey Species

Wolves prey primarily on large ungulates, namely moose, elk, deer, caribou, mountain goat, sheep, muskoxen and bison. Eastern wolves, which are smaller than grey wolves, rely more on smaller deer species and smaller mammals. When ungulates are limited or hunts have been unsuccessful, wolves rely on beaver. Wolves will also fish if the opportunity presents itself—the rainforest wolves of coastal BC fish for salmon, and Bob Bromely, a researcher in the Northwest Territories, observed a wolf successfully preying upon fish in the Talston River, catching five in 15 minutes.

Wolves in a specific habitat tend to have one main prey species. For example, bison are the main prey in northern Alberta near Wood Buffalo National Park, even though deer and moose are also present; elk are preferred in Banff National Park. Even when prey species overlap, certain wolf populations seem to specialize on one prey species.

In the Rocky Mountains, mountain sheep and mountain goats add to the diet. On the boreal prairies, there are bison. Elk only range from BC to Ontario. Hares are a main prey source in Labrador but are not really sought after in zeal elsewhere. Muskoxen are prey for wolves in the arctic mainland and on some of the archipelago islands, and Dall's sheep are additional prey in the Yukon.

Diets also change seasonally. Game species may be migratory, moving to higher or lower elevations or latitudes during summer and winter. In the spring, wolves more commonly prey upon ungulate calves and fawns than adults, because the young can be separated from the adults who protect them. In the winter, wolves prey on yearlings and fully mature ungulates.

Where large prey are present year round, such as in the boreal forest, wolves only rarely go for animals smaller than beaver. However, wolves are opportunistic and will take advantage of small quarry when necessary, including hares, small rodents (mice, voles, ground squirrels, muskrats, lemmings), birds, fish and even foxes, as well as eggs or even small amounts of grass and other vegetable matter. These smaller morsels offer a low caloric return on the energy invested, particularly to feed an entire pack; small prey animals are supplementary but cannot be a permanent substitute for large game species.

Table 2: Main Large Prey Species

	moose	sheep	beaver	caribou	elk	goat	musk-oxen	deer	bison
BC	x	x	x	x	x	x	-	x	
AB	x	x	x	x	x	x		x	x
SK	x		x	x	x			x	x
MB	x		x	x	x			x	x
ON	x		x	x	x			x	
QC	x		x	x				x	
Lab	x		x	x			x		
YK	x	x	x	x	x	x		x	
NWT&NU	x	x	x	x		x	x		x

There are a few contentious prey species of wolves in Canada; these animals and a summary of their management in Canada are described in the following pages. Prey species information has been collated from the most recent available statistics from the relevant government agencies.

Caribou

The caribou feeds the wolf, but it is the wolf who keeps the caribou strong.

–an Inuit saying from the Kivalliq Region

Also known as reindeer, caribou (*Rangifer tarandus*) are divided into two major groups: tundra and woodland caribou. There are several races, considered by some people to be subspecies, of this widely distributed large ungulate across North America and Greenland. Three of these subspecies or races are recognized in Canada: woodland caribou (*R. t. caribou*) and the tundra-inhabiting Peary caribou (*R. t. pearyi*) and barren-ground caribou (*R. t. groenlandicus*), with the Porcupine or Grant's caribou (*R. t. granti*) typically considered one of several distinct herds of barren-ground caribou rather than a separate subspecies or race. Their primary food source is ground and tree lichen; caribou are the only large mammal able to metabolize lichen owing to specialized bacteria and protozoa in their gut.

Barren-ground caribou (females weigh 90 kg, males 150 kg) inhabit the tundra across the entire width of Canada's north from Alaska to Baffin Island, and also live in western Greenland.

They are famous for their massive migratory herds, some numbering in the hundreds of thousands, moving seasonally from the tundra to the taiga, following the same routes for as long as human memory can confirm. Barren-ground caribou are the largest population of caribou, approximately 1.2 million, which is about equal to the population of the other subspecies combined. Barren-ground caribou are divided into eight migratory herds throughout their Canadian range: the Porcupine herd (found in the Yukon as well as Alaska); the Cape Bathurst, Bluenose West, Bluenose East and Bathurst herds (in northern Northwest Territories and western Nunavut); the Ahiak herd (in the Northwest Territories); the Beverly herd (located primarily in Saskatchewan and the Northwest Territories, with portions in Nunavut, Manitoba and Alberta); and the Qamanirjuaq herd (located primarily in Manitoba and Nunavut, with portions in the southeastern Northwest Territories and northeastern Saskatchewan). The Porcupine caribou have a population some 125,000 strong, up to 165,000 some years, migrating annually over 2500 km between their wintering grounds and summer calving grounds, the longest annual land migration of any terrestrial mammal on Earth. The Gwich'in First Nations, the people of the Porcupine River these caribou are named for, relied on the caribou for sustenance, following them for centuries until their nomadic lifestyles ceased in recent years. Wolf numbers on the central barrens have been in decline directly related to declines in Bathurst caribou numbers.

In addition to these major herds, about 120,000 head of caribou comprising several smaller herds remain on the tundra year round, half of them solely on Baffin Island. Many of the herds move to coastal areas for part of the year, such as the Dolphin and Union population, which migrates between the mainland and Victoria Island crossing the Dolphin and Union Strait. This population was once thought to be extinct but at the last population census in 1997 was estimated to be about 28,000 head, ranking it as a species of special concern by the Committee on the Status of Endangered Wildlife in

Caribou Range

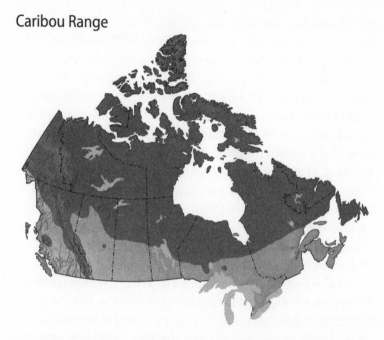

Canada (COSEWIC) in 2004. The warming polar climate and increased shipping across the strait makes ice crossings increasingly dangerous. These caribou are also heavily hunted by local people. The main natural predator of barren-ground caribou is the arctic wolf, which will follow barren-ground herds in their migrations.

Peary caribou are smaller (females weigh 60 kg, males 110 kg) than barren-ground caribou and are pale coloured. They are a Canadian endemic species, found only on the islands of Nunavut and the Northwest Territories in the Canadian Arctic Archipelago. Peary caribou consume less lichen and more moss than other species of caribou, but they forage on any form of available flora in the short growing season of the polar desert. They live in small groups limited by food availability. Peary caribou have endangered species status (COSEWIC 2004). In the past few decades alone, over three-quarters of the population has been lost in a catastrophic die-off attributed to severe ice episodes: thick ice covered the vegetation, and the animals starved to death. Climate change is attributed as causing these previously uncommon melting–freezing ice conditions, which are expected to continue.

Wolves, bears, coyotes, cougars, lynx and humans prey on Peary caribou and, according to the Species at Risk Act (SARA) registry, "While there is nothing to indicate that wolves have caused a significant reduction of these caribou populations, their potential impact is considerably greater now that caribou numbers have reached such a low level." Hunting restrictions are voluntary (the Inuit and Inuvialuit people retain their rights to hunt Peary caribou for subsistence purposes, including within protected areas). The Peary caribou population has continued to decline since population monitoring began in the early 1960s, and the subspecies is at imminent risk of extinction.

In the Northwest Territories, the Peary caribou count on Banks Island dropped from 12,000 in 1972 to 1018 in 1992, but has remained stable at 1000 since. Northwestern Victoria Island (Minto Inlet) had a count of 4500 in 1980 that dropped to a mere 100 in 1993, bouncing back with an estimated population of possibly 500 in 1998, then down to 66 in 2005 and back up to 150 in 2010. The western Queen Elizabeth Islands counted 19,400 in 1961, which dropped to 1080 by 1997, a 94% decline over 36 years that is attributed to consecutive unusually severe winters. A combination of harvesting and harsh winters contributed to the declines on Banks and Victoria Islands. According to the government, the impact of wolf predation on the caribou is unknown because there is little information on wolf numbers. Severe winters are considered the major factor negatively impacting the herds. Another factor that may influence the caribou population is competition for graze with muskoxen.

Woodland (or mountain) caribou are the largest caribou subspecies (females weigh 90–135 kg, males 180–270 kg) and have the darkest colouring. These animals do not form vast herds, but rather remain in smaller groups, and do not make extensive migrations. Their main food source is tree lichen, which is generally associated with wetlands and peatlands of old-growth black and white spruce and tamarack forests and is absent from clear-cuts or sites dominated by shrubs or aspen and poplar stands. It takes 80–150 years for a forest to grow adequate biomass of tree lichen for caribou populations in Alberta and Saskatchewan, and 200–350 years for these forests to mature in British Columbia, so deforestation or tree farming is a big problem for caribou. Woodland caribou depend on these mature old-growth forests during the long, cold Canadian winters because lichen comprise up to 70% of the caribou's diet when succulent grasses and forbs are unavailable. They also require larger tracts of the forest habitat to spread out and avoid predators and human hunters. Loss of habitat is bad news for caribou: forests are cleared for agriculture and logging or by forest fire, and habitats are fragmented by roads, timber cut-blocks, pipelines, oil and gas well-sites, exploration lines and housing developments. Mature forests are also less favoured by moose and deer, and moose and deer attract wolves. If caribou are forced to inhabit younger forests where moose and deer (and therefore wolves) are more frequent, they will not only have to compete for forbs and grasses but will also be more vulnerable to predation.

Nationwide population estimates have only rarely been tallied. The Canadian woodland caribou population was estimated at 193,000 in 1982, but it is declining. Woodland caribou have a patchy distribution, with specific populations identified by COSEWIC and recognized in some provinces and territories as ecotypes. These five distinct populations are based upon geographic location, habitat and behaviour: Newfoundland, Atlantic-Gaspésie, boreal, northern mountain and southern mountain.

The Newfoundland population is not at risk and has a stable population.

The endangered (COSEWIC 2002) Atlantic-Gaspésie population of Quebec is a relic herd of the last remaining maritime woodland caribou along the south and east of the St. Lawrence.

The boreal population or ecotype is the most widespread. The immense boreal forest hosts these caribou across Canada from Newfoundland to British Columbia (*R. t. dawsoni,* once present on the Queen Charlotte Islands, is now extinct) and from the northern treeline once as far south as across the Canada–US border. The boreal woodland caribou remain in forested habitats year round, though they undertake shorter seasonal migrations in search of food between seasons. As a population, they are classified as threatened (COSEWIC 2002) across their current range, with population decline attributed to habitat loss.

In eastern Canada, from Manitoba to Quebec, habitat degradation has allowed white-tailed deer to expand into caribou areas. This situation has resulted in the spread of meningeal brain worm, which is harmless to deer but fatal to caribou. Since the 1970s, government and scientific reports, consultations and recovery plans have concluded that the industrial effects on forests and wildlife are the root cause of caribou decline. Of the two sub-ecotypes in Ontario, the forest-tundra and the forest-dwelling types, the latter has lost 50% of its range (at a rate of 35,000 km^2 per decade), according to the Canadian Parks and Wilderness Society (CPAWS). The forest-tundra woodland caribou, approximately 16,000 head strong along the Hudson Bay and James Bay coasts in northern Ontario, are not deemed to be at risk by COSEWIC.

In the Northwest Territories, the boreal population is stable and estimated at 6000–7000 animals, but heavy truck traffic on highways and winter roads causes increased collisions. Roads and seismic lines also make it easier for predators such as wolves to penetrate the forest and find prey. A hunting quota on non-native resident hunters allows only one woodland caribou (either boreal or northern mountain, but not both) to be harvested per year; non-residents can only hunt woodland caribou in the Mackenzie Mountains. There is no limit or closed season on boreal caribou for aboriginal hunters, and harvest numbers are not recorded.

Some boreal herds exist over ranges spanning the borders of the Northwest Territories and the Yukon, such as the Redstone and Bonnet Plume herds, each estimated to be at least 5000 animals. The total Yukon population is around 25,000 woodland caribou scattered in 17 isolated herds across the territory. The Chisana herd (in Kluane Wildlife Sanctuary in the Yukon and Wrangell–St. Elias National Park in Alaska) is protected from hunting since the herd size declined from 1800 animals in 1989 to less than 700 animals in 2003. Captive rearing was used to try to stabilize the herd, which is now estimated at 720 (2010) with a younger overall age profile.

There are two populations of mountain (woodland) caribou: southern mountain and northern mountain. The northern mountain population comprises 36 herds throughout the Northwest Territories, the Yukon and northern BC. There are approximately 45,000 caribou within these northern mountain ranges (numbers in the Northwest Territories are unknown). The northern mountain population, with a status of special concern (COSEWIC 2002) is doing a bit better than its southern counterpart, which is threatened (COSEWIC 2002). Southern mountain caribou inhabit the Rocky Mountains of west-central Alberta and BC and are simply called the mountain ecotype in these two provinces. In Alberta, the mountain ecotype is somewhat migratory, travelling approximately 80 km between the forested foothills in the winter to the higher elevations of the Rocky Mountains in the summer.

The southern mountain population of woodland caribou is particularly vulnerable because, in addition to unregulated over-hunting in the past, caribou habitat is becoming increasingly fragmented, isolating herds into smaller subpopulations. For example, the Little Smokey herd in Alberta is only about 60–100 individual caribou, designated as threatened provincially in 1985 and nationally in 2001 (CPAWS): the decline has become one of the most contentious wildlife issues in the province. Other herds inhabit various regions of Canada, but many, such as the Little Smokey, are isolated from other herds and as a subpopulation face extinction, making any loss to that herd unsustainable. The provincial woodland caribou population estimate in the 1960s was 7000–9000 but has seen sharp decline ever since, estimated at 2935 in 2010 (CPAWS). According to the 1991 Alberta Management Plan, the caribou population decline is "related to high harvest levels, predation, loss of habitat, and the disturbances associated with changing land use."

Albertans are well aware of the rapid and constant increase of logging and oil and gas extraction, particularly the infamous Alberta tar sands. Agriculture, timber harvesting and especially oil and gas development have caused vast habitat changes and loss of the northern boreal forest (new roads, seismic lines, pipelines, pipeline right-of-ways cleared, deforestation). Boreal woodland caribou using areas near roads and seismic lines are more vulnerable to harvest and predation. In November 2009, the Alberta government, in its "Action Plan for West-Central Alberta Caribou Recovery," authorized ongoing logging and oil and gas development in critical caribou habitat north of Hinton and Grande Cache, while management proposals to restore and balance woodland caribou and moose numbers in Alberta have been to cull wolf numbers. Hunting restrictions of caribou have been mostly voluntary on behalf of the hunters. Moose hunting was not halted because moose draw in the wolves, and the means of determining the unknown status of the moose population is by hunters bringing the jaw bones of the moose to Fish and Wildlife. According to Robichaud, hundreds of wolves have been killed in a 5000 km² area in west-central Alberta since 2005, mainly by aerial hunting and strychnine poisoning.

On the other side of the Rockies, BC's caribou have dwindled from 2500 in 1995 to approximately 1900 in 2007. Declines owe to clear-cut logging of old-growth habitat over a 10,000 km² area near Quesnel. In 2007 the BC government announced a plan to recover its mountain caribou population back to sustainable levels by protecting 2.2 million hectares of habitat from road building and logging, with a growth of 380,000 hectares in protected forest—not contiguous forest, however, but in various areas in accordance with recommendations by the timber companies. Conservationists are concerned that the plan focuses on winter habitat at higher elevations while spring habitat in lowlands remains the heaviest hit—and most highly desired by the timber companies. In addition to setting aside land, the recovery plan calls for responsible management of snowmobiling, heli-skiing and cat-skiing in caribou habitat, which could imply legally closing some areas from these activities. The government stated that it will put forward $75,000 to develop snowmobiling opportunities outside of herd areas. One interesting proposal was to develop maternity pens cooperatively with First Nations in the area to protect newborns and calves.

Another step of the caribou recovery plan in BC is to increase wolf and cougar harvest levels and includes sterilization of wolves and culling of individual wolves or entire packs. The Ministry of Environment culls wolves to ease predation on caribou, with the timber industry co-funding the management program. Hundreds of thousands of dollars have been spent since 2001 funding the cull. The Ministry released a statement in 2007 reporting that 41 wolves had been killed in the 10,000 km^2 area since 2002, while caribou numbers increased from 30 to 40 animals. Wolf densities in the area are naturally around 9.6–9.8 animals per 1000 km^2; culling has brought down densities to as low as 5.4 per 1000 km^2. A temporary suspension in the cull between March 2004 and November 2005 from a lack of funding saw the wolf population bounce back to its original density. In sum, caribou populations are not recovering relative to the number of wolves killed, and culling would have to endlessly continue at the cost of hundreds of thousands of dollars and no moratorium on timber extraction in the area.

Studies indicate that caribou cows move to higher elevations to remove themselves from habitats with high wolf–moose activity in BC's mountains. They also move away from wolf–moose activity in the boreal and mixed forests of northeastern Alberta. Moose are the primary prey of wolves in the boreal forest and are more abundant in well-drained upland forest; caribou confine themselves to black spruce bogs and fens. Wolves are the principal predator of caribou, next to grizzly bears and cougars. However, wolf populations are more directly tied to moose availability. Researchers suggest that human management has caused a flip in the system. Formerly there were high caribou, moderate wolf and low moose numbers, but deforestation and wolf culling have resulted in low caribou and high moose numbers.

Boreal forest habitat loss in the past 10–15 years has escalated with agricultural conversion and deforestation from the timber and energy industries. Scientists concur that industrial development has increased predation rates. Seismic cutlines create linear features that improve wolves' access to prey, as can recreational land use, particularly snowmobiles and ski trails. Cutblocks create early seral habitat of young shrubs and forbs that are the first plants to appear after clearing, and these areas increase moose and deer densities. And according to the BC Ministry of Environment, "When moose expand into areas occupied by caribou, wolf populations also increase, which increases the potential for predation on caribou."

So, while habitat loss remains the primary cause of caribou declines, the wolf is being culled as the primary method of saving caribou. Yet, as explicitly stated in the Alberta government's own Alberta Woodland Caribou Recovery Plan (2005), "Ultimately, habitat conservation and management is the fundamental tool to reduce undue predation on caribou... Predator control will not succeed as a sole, or predominant, tool for caribou recovery." The Alberta government continues to sell mineral and timber leases in this area. It begs one to ask why the government bothers funding expensive conservation reports when they are going to completely ignore the solutions that the experts write within them.

Elk

I do not think it is possible to truly understand even one leg muscle of one elk in the absence of wolves...the size and endurance of hoofed beast...their speed, coordination, and quicksilver reactions...wolves sang these things into their present form.

–Douglas Chadwick, *The Kingdom*

The American elk (*Cervus elaphus*), also known as wapiti in Canada, is the same species as the Eurasian red deer. There were formerly six subspecies in North America, but two (*C. e. merriumi* and *C. e. canadensis*) have gone extinct since European settlement. Three of the current four subspecies are in Canada: the Rocky Mountain elk (*C. e. nelsoni*), the Roosevelt elk (*C. e. roosevelti*) and the Manitoba elk (*C. e. manitobensis*). The endangered tule elk is endemic to

California. Elk is an important prey species of wolves in parts of Canada, and this large game species has seen significant population declines in parts of its range. It once ranged from BC east to Quebec and north through the boreal forest. Settlement of the Canadian prairies combined with over-hunting deprived elk herds of their habitat and extirpated them from much of their range. However, scattered populations continue to exist throughout the forest regions skirting the prairies and in the mountains of the west. The most recent population estimate of elk in Canada is about 72,000 (2010).

The Rocky Mountain elk is the most abundant subspecies in North America. Owing to their ability to adapt to diverse habitats, Rocky Mountain elk have been introduced throughout various habitats across both Canada and the United States to replenish decimated populations. Elk populations were at their lowest in the early 20th century, as was the situation with most Canadian large mammals as a result of over-hunting and habitat loss. Between 1917 and 1920, Banff and Jasper National Parks received several hundred elk from Yellowstone National Park in the US. Wolves were exterminated from Banff National Park and elk populations subsequently boomed. In the 1930s, Ontario received elk subsidies to replenish its last two herds surviving in the Burwash/French River area, as did the Yukon, northwest of Whitehorse, and BC, to the Queen Charlotte Islands, in the 1950s. Elk have also become a common sight in agricultural areas as semi-domesticated livestock for meat, hides and antler velvet, the latter for reputed medicinal benefit. In the Canadian Rockies, Alberta hosts a population of about 20,000–25,000 (2008) Rocky Mountain elk, mainly in Banff, Jasper and Waterton Lakes National Parks and adjacent foothills, with an additional scattered population in the central parkland region, Elk Island National Park, which is a strong player in the conservation of elk in Canada. Elk Island was established in 1906 as a reserve to protect a small herd of endangered elk. Today there

Elk Range

are over 1000 elk, as well as bison, moose and white-tailed deer, thriving in the 200 km² fenced-in sanctuary and research area. Elk from this population are stock for reintroductions elsewhere, such as to various areas in Ontario in 1998 and 2001, including Lake of the Woods, the north shore of Lake Huron, Bancroft–North Hastings and Nipissing–French River. On the west side of the Rockies, BC has twice as many elk as Alberta, mainly in the Kootenays and the Peace–Omineca region, which make up over half of Canada's total population of wild Rocky Mountain elk.

BC also has a small population of Roosevelt elk. Roosevelt elk are the largest subspecies of elk, with males weighing in at over 400 kg and females around 250 kg. This subspecies lives only on Vancouver Island and pockets of coastline on the BC mainland, with a population of about 3600 individuals (2003); the majority (about 3300) are on Vancouver Island and have been isolated from the rest of the population long enough to be of a single monophyletic lineage. Human settlement, loss of old-growth forest and over-hunting extirpated the elk from most of its range in coastal BC and on other gulf islands. Reports from original settlers state that the elk were abundant in the early 1800s but rare by the end of that century. Predation rates on calves are not comprehensively known; wolves, black bears and cougars (the greatest concentration of cougars in North America is on Vancouver Island) are predators of elk, but black-tailed deer on the island are the main ungulate prey species for these predators.

From the 1920s to the 1970s, BC wildlife officials attempted to exterminate wolves from Vancouver Island, where wolves had appeared through natural migration. Sport hunters complained that wolf predation on black-tailed deer was reducing their hunting success. Elk (Roosevelt subspecies) hunting has been restricted on Vancouver Island on and off since 1909 but is still ongoing. Black-tailed deer numbers are declining, partially owing to increased logging depleting habitat, which leads to increased predation rates on elk; in addition, if elk are unable to find suitable habitat and productive, uncrowded range, they become more susceptible to predation, particularly in the winter.

The Manitoba elk was originally found from the eastern edge of the Rocky Mountains east to Manitoba, but today survives only in the provincial and national parks of Manitoba and eastern Saskatchewan. Despite being called Manitoba elk, Saskatchewan has almost three-quarters of the population, which mostly inhabits the southern fringe of the boreal forest north of Prince Albert and the Moose Mountain, Cypress Hills and Duck Mountain areas in the south of the province. Manitoba has a herd distributed in and around Riding Mountain National Park.

Moose

What the Buffalo was to the Plains, the Whitetail Deer to the Southern woods, and the Caribou to the Barrens, the Moose is to this great Northern belt of swamp and timberland...It is the creature that enables the natives to live.

–Ernest Thompson Seton, *Lives of Game Animals*

The moose (*Alces alces*) is an iconic Canadian species and a remarkable-looking animal. Moose antlers are among the largest of all cervids in the world, expanding to a 1.8 m spread and weighing up to 32 kg. Adult males can obtain a robust weight of over 800 kg, and body length measures 2.3–2.8 m, with heights of 1.8 m to the shoulder; females weigh 330–496 kg and are slightly smaller in stature. A truly boreal species, the moose does not range far from the massive forest belt. Black and grizzly bears prey heavily on young moose calves, as do cougars and even wolverines, particularly in the Yukon and perhaps the Northwest Territories, where moose are at the edge of their northern range; but it is the wolf that is the moose's main predator.

The very close predator–prey relationship between moose and wolves has been studied on Isle Royale for decades. When moose numbers are high, wolves act as a culling agent for old or diseased animals. Wolves can also take healthy calves and adult moose year round, but a single wolf is no match against a healthy adult moose. It takes four or five wolves to take down this large animal that is equipped with lethal antlers and long, strong, kicking legs. It is dangerous and difficult for wolves to prey on moose; many wolves die of injuries from moose hooves and antlers. Statistically, only one in 12 attempts by wolves to take down an adult moose is successful. Despite its gangly appearance, a moose can run up to 50 km per hour. The moose's long legs also allow it to travel in deep snow more easily than most other ungulates. Typically, it is when the moose becomes trapped in deep snow (over 90 cm) or mud that the wolves gain an advantage. Deep snow also causes moose to yard together in greater numbers, making them more vulnerable to wolves. Crusted snow can be a nasty impediment to the moose's ability to move, cutting and piercing the skin on the forelegs and even cracking the hooves. These injuries weaken the animal, and the blood draws the attention of wolves. On firm ground, a strong adult moose has two choices: fight or flee. Fleeing is usually the more fatal option: a moose cannot outrun a wolf, and a pack of wolves will bite and tear at its quarry, weakening it with injury and blood loss until it cannot run any farther or fight any longer.

Moose are an important game species for hunters across the country and for trophy hunters who come from abroad, as well as a significant subsistence species for many native communities. With the exception of PEI, moose are found in all provinces and territories in Canada. There are four subspecies in North America. The northwestern moose (*A. a. andersoni*) ranges from BC to Ontario (with an introduced population in Cape Breton) and through the Yukon and the Northwest Territories, then gives way to the eastern moose (*A. a. americana*), whose range extends to Maine, mainland Nova Scotia (where they are an endangered species), New Brunswick and Quebec. The Alaskan moose (*A. a. gigas*) ranges into the Yukon and northwestern BC, and the Shiras moose (*A. a. shirasi*) is mostly found in the US Rockies but takes a few lanky strides over the border into southeastern BC. Moose from Elk Island National Park were introduced to Cape Breton Island in 1947–48, after being extirpated from the island by the early 1900s.

The population estimate of moose in Canada is a rough one, between 500,000 and a million, and it endures significant hunting by humans. For example, the Northwest Territories claims approximately 20,000 moose at the edge of the northern boreal range, with an estimated moose harvest of 1000–2000 moose per year.

Moose throughout the country suffer from parasites and their related diseases, such as brain worm from deer. They can be so relentlessly attacked by ticks that they rub their fur off against trees; areas of fur damage and loss result in a pale grey appearance that gives these animals the name "ghost moose." Losing fur over the course of a summer plus significant blood loss does not bode well for moose enduring a cold Canadian winter. A major tick infestation in moose in the 1980s and 1990s in Alberta caused a high moose mortality rate. Few moose die of old age.

Moose Range

Bison

Plains bison

What is life?
It is the flash of a firefly in the night.
It is the breath of a buffalo in the winter time.
It is the little shadow which runs across the grass
And loses itself in the Sunset.

–Crowfoot (1890), in *Native American Wisdom*

There is debate as to whether plains and wood bison (*Bison bison*) are subspecies of the American bison. Bulls and cows of both ecotypes have short black horns, which curve inward on the males, but are straight on the females. The males, weighing 350–1000 kg and standing 1.7–1.8 m tall at the shoulder, are larger than the females. Wood bison are generally taller and less stocky than plains bison. Historically, the Canadian range of wood bison was throughout the boreal forest of BC, Alberta, the Northwest Territories and the Yukon.

Wood bison

Incredibly, a wolf of only 50 kg can take down a bison weighing up to 1000 kg. Group strategy and often—but not always—a predatory advantage over a bison's disadvantage (injury, illness or getting trapped in snow, mud or water) allows a few tenacious wolves to take down a seemingly impossible victim. It may take several days after the initial attack to injure and weaken the victim before the wolves can succeed without risking their own lives. Bison calves are more often preyed upon than adults, as is the case with all ungulate prey species. In Wood Buffalo National Park, the wolves' preferred prey is bison. Carbyn observed 65 wolf–bison encounters in Wood Buffalo National Park during his studies; only 17 of those resulted in attacks, and only three resulted in kills. He also observed wolves resting nearby the bison, which seemed unperturbed by the wolves' presence. Carbyn hypothesized either that the wolves felt comfortable being near to their potential prey, or that the wolves were using the nearby group of bulls as a decoy to encourage large cow–calf herds to approach the bulls without realizing the danger.

Plains bison are the iconic species of the prairies and plains. We all know the stories of how they once roamed the landscape in immense numbers until the white man came along. Before that, the prairie wolf, or buffalo wolf, was the bison's main predator—and obviously the wolf had no negative impact on the bison's population. The early European settlers hunted the plains bison to near extinction, partly out of greed for fur and partly out of an obtuse strategy to expropriate the native peoples, and sought to tame the wild landscape by exterminating the wolves. Hit with an onslaught of shotguns and strychnine, the wolves didn't have much to live for with the bison gone anyway, and the 19th century's massacres of bison and wolves saw the demise of both species on the prairies.

Only in what was to become Wood Buffalo National Park in northwestern Alberta did both wolves and bison remain. In the early 20th century, bison became a national treasure, and the Canadian government purchased the largest plains bison herd from a Montana rancher named Michel Pablo and transferred it to an area near Wainwright, AB. Apparently the herd was established from only six motherless calves—legend has it that they were the last survivors of the Blackfoot Indian hunt in Montana and had followed Samuel Walking Coyote's horses back to camp. The Wainwright herd established and grew in numbers, creating Wainwright Buffalo Park, and between 1925 and 1928, 6673 plains bison were transferred to Wood Buffalo National Park. Tragically, not only would these bison hybridize with the existing wood bison in the park, but the introduced animals had been in contact with domestic cattle and brought brucellosis and tuberculosis to the wild bison still remaining in Alberta.

Wood bison never had the massive herds of the plains bison; population estimates pre-1900 are uncertain, but numbers suggest that there once were over 168,000 wood bison in Canada.

They were hunted almost to extinction during the 19th century; habitat loss, severe winters and anthrax outbreaks as well as brucellosis and tuberculosis caused additional declines in the population, down to an estimated low of 250 animals by 1893. By 1922 they had recovered to nearly 2000 individuals, at which time Wood Buffalo National Park was established to protect the wood bison and their habitat.

Owing to a newfound protectionism of endangered bison during the reintroduction phases, any losses caused by wolf depredation were hard to stomach. After the return of bison to the plains, few people wanted to see them eaten by wolves. Wolf control was considered a duty. Even though human error and greed caused the demise of the bison, wolves were culled in Alberta for threatening bison numbers. Wolf control programs began in the 1930s and increased in the 1940s when reports of wolves killing bison reached the public media.

By 1940 the wood bison were feared extinct owing to inbreeding with plains bison. Then, in 1957, a small herd of about 200 pure wood bison was discovered hiding in the trees in the Nyarling River area of Wood Buffalo National Park. After extensive analysis of skulls and skins, it was determined that these animals were the only bison representative of the original pre-1925 wood bison remaining in North America.

A recovery program was established in 1957, and it proved successful. In 1963, 18 head from the Nyarling River herd were captured and transferred east of Great Slave Lake, where they would become the Mackenzie bison herd. The Mackenzie herd, which is now about 1600 animals, is the world's largest free-ranging herd of disease-free wood bison. In 1965, slightly over 20 head from the Nyarling River herd were transferred to Elk Island National Park, where in 1975 this herd became the source for a subsequent recovery program. Thirty of the Elk Island bison have been relocated as far away as the Lenski Stolby Nature Park near Yakutsk, Sahka Republic, Russia, to ensure global security of wood bison in a geographically separate population.

Bison Range

Today, there are herds of wood bison in Alberta, Manitoba, British Columbia and the Yukon, with the majority of free-roaming wood bison in the southwestern Northwest Territories. There are several large independent herds: the Mackenzie herd, the Nahanni herd (in Liard Valley between Fort Liard and Nahanni Butte, extending south into British Columbia), the Hook Lake and Little Buffalo herds (Slave River lowlands) and several herds in Wood Buffalo National Park. Statistics from 2006 estimate that 4188 wood bison survive in seven wild, established, disease-free herds and 6216 in four wild, established herds that are positive for either tuberculosis or brucellosis. Over 1000 bison are in captive breeding and research programs. While plains bison are domesticated and raised as cattle throughout the prairies, Saskatchewan hosts a free-ranging herd of plains bison in Prince Albert National Park.

Continued threats to wood bison are the persistence of brucellosis and tuberculosis in bison herds of both wood and plains bison, the cross breeding of the two ecotypes and habitat loss (development of cities, industries, agriculture, forestry, oil and gas).

Muskoxen

*It is glorious
when the great musk oxen
down there, glossy, black,
cluster in small groups
to face and watch the dogs.*

–"Old Song of the Musk Ox People" [Inuit],
Native American Songs and Poems: An Anthology

Standing 1.5 m tall to the shoulder and weighing 270–315 kg, with a massive, thick hide of dense fur, an adult bull muskox (*Ovibos moschatus*) is formidable prey for a wolf, the only wild predator of muskoxen. Cow muskoxen are slightly smaller (1.2 m tall and up to 225 kg) but still massive mammals. The strategy of the wolf is to take advantage of some vulnerability; in the case of muskoxen, this vulnerability would be being separated from the herd. The muskox's strategy is to stand off threats in a defence formation. The dominant bull faces the threat with the other members of the herd in close ranks behind him, or they form a tight circle, with large adults facing outward to the threat and calves or weaker individuals safe within the circle. This defence strategy works very well against wolves, which will eventually give up. Only if an individual becomes separated from the herd can wolves harass it to exhaustion and bring it down.

Muskoxen can survive on the almost-barren tundra feeding on mainly grasses, sedges and lichen, as well as riparian willows. They can endure the incessantly long, cold and dark winters with temperatures typically between -40° C and -20° C thanks to their thick woolly coats. The wool layer of the coat is stronger and significantly warmer than sheep's wool and supposedly finer than cashmere; the Inuit call the wool *qiviut*, and they call the muskoxen *omingmak*—"the animal with skin like a beard."

In Canada, more than 85,000 muskoxen (and perhaps over 100,000, fluctuating seasonally and annually) live on the mainland and arctic islands of Nunavut and the Northwest Territories. Small herds live in the northern Yukon, and there is a free-roaming, introduced herd in northern Quebec.

Muskoxen Range

In the Northwest Territories, muskoxen live primarily on Banks Island, with significant populations on Ellesmere and Victoria Islands. Numbers are so high on Banks (70,000 non-calf individuals in 2001) that there is concern that they are threatening food sources for caribou.

Muskoxen numbers have recovered from near devastation between the 1820s and 1917, when the animal was finally given federal protected status, banning trade in hides. Muskoxen had become an important food source for coastal Inuit communities, whose populations were growing and requiring them to travel further inland for additional hunting opportunities. At the same time a new fashion in Europe called for thousands of hides to be made into sleigh robes. Europeans (apparently explorers and whalers) killed thousands of muskoxen for fresh meat and to export these hides. Muskoxen are easy quarry for humans: they do not range far and are easily located. Once found, they don't flee, but assume the defence strategy that works so well against natural predators such as the wolf, but is tragically suicidal against human hunters with guns. Many herds were hunted to extinction.

The 19th century marked the demise of many mammals in Canada. There was an increased human population through natural growth as well as immigration, a vital fur trade within the country as well as abroad to the fashion-hungry Europeans, and the introduction of guns to a formerly trapping and bow-hunting heritage. By 1967, muskoxen populations on some northern islands had recovered enough to withstand a managed hunt for Inuit communities. However, some populations have not been reproducing for several subsequent years, causing their populations to continuously decline.

OTHER INTERSPECIES RELATIONSHIPS

Carrion left by wolves feeds many other animals, such as birds of prey, foxes and even bears, that cannot hunt large ungulates the way a pack of wolves can, or that cannot open a carcass the way a large predator can. When prey is abundant, wolves will take down more than they need and tolerate other species feeding on their kills. For example, Thayer documented seven wolves take down two Porcupine caribou and feed on both. Then they all moved to one of the carcasses, liberating the second for a watching grizzly and a bunch of ravens to feed on. After 20 minutes, the wolves finished feeding, licked themselves clean and rolled about in the grass. Then they chased off the bear and birds and reclaimed the second caribou carcass, tearing off large chunks to take back to the den. The leftovers were then abandoned for the grizzly, ravens, eagles, magpies, foxes or whatever other animals wanted a share. This interspecies sharing is one way wolves benefit other species unable to take down large prey. If there were no wolves to take down a large ungulate, it would be a detriment to the health and survival rates of many other animals such as bears and foxes. These scavengers must politely wait their turn, though: in many cases when scavengers—foxes, bears, wolverines, etc.—come to the table too early, they become part of the menu.

In the arctic, interspecies sharing benefits the wolves that follow around polar bears, which are the only predator able to hunt seal. Arctic wolves rely upon seal carrion, as do arctic foxes. Thayer observed this strategy on two occasions: one involved six bears being followed by five wolves and numerous foxes; another involved 13 polar bears being followed by four wolves. Wolves in arctic regions abandon a territorial hunting strategy and rely on a nomadic pattern, following the polar bears like arctic foxes do. Members of the same wolf pack spread out over several square kilometres as they follow several polar bears. This strategy aims at procuring more seals for the pack.

Predation by wolves on southern fox species is rare, but in Canada's high arctic, the arctic fox that follows polar bears for scavenging prey, just as wolves do, is frequently preyed upon by wolves—so much so that the arctic fox is considered a regular prey species of arctic wolves. Prey is scarce in the far north, so no source of meat is ignored. Foxes, with their scavenging nature, are in direct competition with wolves in this habitat.

Ravens also scavenge wolf kills and follow wolves around for these opportunities. Wolves in turn also watch for ravens raucously signalling the locations of other sources of carrion. There is interspecies competition at kill sites as well. Large numbers of ravens can harass wolves off the carcass. A large pack of wolves deals better with scavengers such as ravens, while a lone wolf would have a more difficult time. Cougars, which are solitary hunters, have been observed being mobbed by ravens at a carcass. More interestingly, wolves and ravens often appear to be interacting in a manner that can be described no other way than playing.

Most wolf–coyote interactions are aggressive in nature, in defence of territory or food or offspring. Where wolves and coyotes overlap in range, wolves not only attack coyotes but also prey upon and eat them. Coyotes scavenge carcasses left by wolves but otherwise avoid wolves altogether and exist where wolves do not.

Information on interspecies relationships between cougars and wolves is rare—cougars being scarce—but it is obvious that the two species do not enjoy each other's company. A cougar is a solitary animal and avoids conflict with other predators, particularly a pack of wolves, which the cougar would have a significant disadvantage of fending off. There are few documented cases of cougars killed by wolves: a cougar was killed by wolves near Glacier National Park in 1990, and there were two other kills in 1993. However, there are many cases where biologists have documented wolves being killed by cougars, typically after the wolves attempted to scavenge cougar kills.

Bycatch is a problem with snaring, similar to fishing. A recent study in Alberta showed that even though it is illegal to trap cougars, cougars were being caught in wolf snares at an increasing rate. Cougars are often caught in snares set for wolves or coyotes, or in large conibears set for lynx, bobcats or wolverines. Trappers have to be very careful in setting snares to mitigate bycatch of non-target species. A radio-collaring experiment conducted through the University of Alberta proved that cougars frequently scavenge carcasses from wolf kills, making them vulnerable to being caught in snares, which trappers commonly set up near wolf kills to harvest wolves. Provincial data showed that accidental snaring was a dramatically increasing cause of cougar mortality over the past 20 years. The mortalities of the radio-collared cougars in the U of A study were 100% human caused, and the addition of snaring mortality added to hunting mortality resulted in low annual survival. Cougars are not trap-shy and are easily caught in these traps. Wolves are more wary.

Wildlife Predators of Wolves

Grizzly bears are probably the most significant predator of wolves. Numerous researchers have witnessed grizzlies digging up wolf dens and killing and eating the pups within. If the pack is attending the den, they will often be successful at driving the bear off and protecting the pups. For this reason, wolves can be aggressive toward bears and will chase and even kill them if they come to close to their dens, or wolves will kill bear cubs if given the opportunity and will even chase unimposing bears. Despite the threats that these predators pose to each other, there are many cases of the two species peacefully coexisting with or at least tolerating each other, as seen in the example of the carcass sharing observed by Thayer (see p. 98). Typically, and understandably, lone wolves will avoid grizzly families and lone grizzlies will avoid packs of wolves.

Black bears and polar bears will also advantageously prey on susceptible wolves, both adult and pup. Bears are extremely opportunistic. Both species defend their offspring from the other. According to Carbyn, "Bears are usually, but not always, dominant over wolves when the two species arrive at a carcass."

Airborne assaults on wolf pups by raptors are also a cause of wolf mortality.

DISEASE

Wolves are susceptible to dozens of diseases and parasites: all sorts of worms from their prey; skin parasites such as mange, mites, ticks and fleas (though external parasites are less problematic in cold northern climates); viruses such as distemper and rabies; bacteria such as bovine tuberculosis (from bison); and even cancers, pneumonia, lyme disease and rickets. Old-timers suffer much as human geriatrics do from cataracts and arthritis. This section describes some of the most common conditions wolves succumb to and those that they are wrongly perceived to carry. It is worthwhile to be aware of some of these conditions to prevent them from spreading within wolf populations, to other wild animals or to pets, particularly dogs.

Rabies is a zoonotic (transmitted by animals) viral disease that causes acute encephalitis (inflammation of the brain) in warm-blooded animals. The virus concentrates in the affected animal's bodily liquids, particularly saliva, which is why the disease is most often transmitted through a bite—or when wolves eat from a shared carcass, spreading the disease through the pack. A bite or scratch punctures the victim's skin, allowing the virus to enter nerve cells that travel to the brain or central nervous system, as well as other organs and muscles. However, there does not need to be a cut or bite: dried saliva on the fur also carries the virus and can come into contact with the mouth, eyes, nostrils or an open sore of another animal or a person. There have been cases of people contracting rabies after being in bat caves, presumably by breathing in guano dust carrying the virus, which then enters the nasal or lung tissues.

Rabid animals display two general forms of behaviour: furious and dumb. The former first affects the brain, making the victim aggressive, viciously combative and unpredictable; the latter first affects the spinal cord, causing displays of lethargy, friendliness and weak limbs, often with the animal unable to raise its head or make sounds owing to paralysis of the throat and neck muscles. The virus causes severe pain in the throats of both animal and human victims when they swallow liquids and makes victims fearful of water, which is why the disease is sometimes referred to as hydrophobia. This choking and dehydration is also what causes the "foaming at the mouth," but it is not always a visible sign. More important is to notice a change in behaviour or unusual behaviour in an animal. It is not normal for a wild wolf or any other wild carnivore to be playful and friendly toward humans; these animals should be avoided and reported to wildlife officials. Death occurs within a few days to a week after the symptoms appear in both forms of rabies; the secondary symptom that causes death is typically respiratory failure.

There is still much paranoia about the idea of rabid wolves, but contrary to this perception, wolves rarely carry rabies. Rabies discovered in foxes and coyotes in Alberta in 1952 resulted in a wolf slaughter over the next four years: 4200 wolves were poisoned and over 50,000 foxes, 35,000 coyotes and 1850 bears were killed by associated non-target poisoning. There is claim that the virus was detected in a single post-mortem wolf; if so, it was likely a lone wolf that had contracted the virus from a dog or a fox. The most common carriers of the disease are cats, dogs, bats, raccoons, skunks, foxes and other small animals. In 1990, John and Mary Theberge, who were doing radio-collaring work on wolves, discovered several post-mortem Algonquin wolves were carriers of the disease. No rabies had been reported throughout the Great Lakes in the decade previous, and haven't been since that time. It is believed that the wolves contracted the disease from foxes scavenging wolf kills.

Mange is a skin disease caused by parasitic mites, common in canines, dogs, wolves and coyotes, but can also affect other animals. It is persistent and contagious. There are two forms of mange: demodectic mange (called demodicosis in humans) and sarcoptic mange. Demodectic mange is caused by *Demodex canis*, a naturally occurring mite in the skin follicles of canines. If the animal's immune system is impaired by stress or malnutrition, the mites can over-reproduce and cause mild to severe skin irritation and inflammation. Eventually, it can kill the animal. These mites live in the pores of the skin and cause little to no itching, but do cause skin lesions, crusting and fur loss. Fur loss will leave a wolf vulnerable to the weather—sun, rain, snow—and can mean death from exposure in the winter. Sarcoptic mange causes intense itching from female mites burrowing under the skin to lay eggs. Shockingly, in Montana in 1909, wolves were captured and deliberately infected with sarcoptic mange, and then re-released into the wild as a wolf-control experiment. Many researchers concur that it was through this ignorant and draconian measure that sarcoptic mange was introduced to the Canadian prairies, where it had never occurred prior to 1909. By the mid-1980s sarcoptic mange was a serious problem in Saskatchewan's wolf population and significantly decreased the population.

Canine parvovirus is a virus that attacks the gastrointestinal system. First discovered in 1978, it is another disease introduced to wild wolf populations by domestic dogs. The symptoms include vomiting and diarrhea, causing the afflicted animal to succumb to dehydration. The disease has had a serious impact on the endangered red wolf in the United States, which is unable to withstand disease outbreaks in its population.

Canine distemper is a microscopic virus, highly contagious among canids. It is not common in the wild, and wolves generally contract it through contact with domestic dogs. A wolf or dog with distemper might display watery discharge from the eyes or nose, diarrhea or, at severe stages, muscle spasms or seizures.

Canadian History with Wolves

What is Canada's history with wolves? Why does the southwestern Canada–US border virtually delineate the range of the grizzly bear, the cougar and the wolf? Were Canadian views of wildlife so different from those of our American neighbours in the days of the early settlers? Are they even so different today? In *Wolf Mountains: A History of Wolves along the Great Divide*, Karen Jones examines the American and Canadian wilderness paradigms. She cites Roderick Nash as claiming in 1968 that Canadians lagged two generations behind Americans in appreciating nature, and park scholar John Ise as postulating that Canada followed America's lead in establishing protected areas (the first national park, for example, was Yellowstone in the US). Yet the greatest extirpation of large North American mammals has occurred in the US, and Canadian wolf reintroduction south of the border has been met with hot resistance. "With the beaver and the maple leaf as naturalistic symbols of their country," Jones explains, "Canadians presented themselves as more respectful of the environment than pioneers south of the border."

Canadians have a quirky sort of nationalism—we don't give it much thought until we are differentiating ourselves from Americans! So, if we are different, or have the chance to be, can we discover our Canadian identity lurking camouflaged in the wilderness of our nation?

It is interesting to consider the history of events during the pioneering of our nation. In the staking and clearing—and civilizing—of the land, extermination of wolves was an unquestionable duty. Wolves were to be responsibly dealt with as if they were a cockroach or rat infestation. Perhaps these actions would have been warranted if there were some ecological justification by early thinkers for eliminating certain species, such as removing exotic species; but wolves were very much a part of the local ecology, simply disliked.

By the 1960s, wolves were mostly gone from the lower 48 states and eastern Canada, but still survived in western and northern Canada. Canadian wolves in the remote North and West had survived largely by virtue of our great, sparsely populated land mass, and as a result of shifts from the fur trade to ranching and from ranching to more urban lifestyles. But another shift occurred as well. Canadians began to recognize the ecological role of all animals, including wolves; Americans were looking back to Canada for wolf reintroduction. How did this perspective of wolves come to change?

FIRST NATIONS

The First Nations who lived on the land we now consider Canada have a history and perception of wildlife, including wolves, filled with respect. They have praised the animal world in their folklore, religion and artwork for generations and believe that all animals have spirits and were participants in the creation of the universe: beaver, deer, cougar, bear, bison, orca and several birds, such as the Canada goose, hummingbird, magpie, hawk, eagle and especially the raven. The Canadian wild dog family is also fully represented: fox, coyote and wolf.

Animals are the pantheon of the pagan religions. They are also symbols of good or bad omens; to see one can be an omen of an event specific to that animal. For example, in some traditions, meeting a deer on a trail is an omen that you will meet a person of the opposite sex who will flirt with you. One would pray to various animal spirits associated with such things as protection, health or fortune.

Each animal is recognized for and identified with its qualities and attributes. Beaver is industrious and hardworking; Bison is strong; Otter is playful and happy; Raccoon is a problem solver; Weasel is cunning, smart, swift and courageous. Among the dogs, Coyote is one of the most important animal spirits, portrayed as either the creator or the trickster. He has many special, even magical, powers and is wise with the teachings of life's lessons. Fox is swift and cunning, considered either a messenger or a trickster. Wolf is commonly attributed with being a protector, a good hunter, wise and intelligent, strong, agile, gregarious, courageous, mysterious and devoted; he is loyal to his mate and family and carries the gift of song. Wolf is often a symbol of love and care for family and cooperation in community. In stories where animals are characters, Wolf is typically a wise leader owed respect.

Wolf is credited with many things, including the creation of other animals. The Seneca tell a tale that credits the wolf for painting the colours on the birds. Wolf is often considered a divinity, coming and going from the spirit world, running down the Milky Way—Canada's Blackfoot call the Milky Way the Wolf Trail. The Cree believed that divine wolves visited Earth when the northern lights shined in the sky.

Shamans and warriors would call upon the wolf for the symbolic and spiritual powers that it possessed. They would perform wolf dances in ceremonies and rituals in honour and recognition of the sacred animal. The Wolf Dance is an important ceremony of many groups, including many West Coast peoples who danced the Wolf Dance in the Winter Ceremony.

Wolf is a common good luck charm for hunters and fishers in most native groups; skilled hunters have wolf spirit guides. Some Pacific Northwest groups credit the wolf with teaching man how to hunt whales. But there are many more

legends about the affinity of the wolf and the whale and their high significance to humans. The native peoples saw many similarities in wolves and orcas, from their colouring to their behaviours. They both live in packs (or pods) and are adept hunters, often hunting as a single unit with group strategy. Some legends claim that the wolf and orca shift freely between the two species, that each is one of the same animal.

The wolf is a *yek* animal. Yek animals may transform their appearance and hold the power of transition to move from one geographic location to another. Many native cultures have a shaman who controls a yek, which is the domain of spiritual animals. The shaman encounters these vital spirits on his vision quests, and people who have died may appear in the form of these animals.

Inuit mythology has a strong symbolism of outer appearances, that fundamentally man and wild animals are brethren with only different skins. This belief is not such a leap of faith since this hunting nation acknowledged how similar the skeletal structures of all mammals are. Once they removed the pelt from a polar bear, they saw the body of a man.

The Inuit also have a mythology of a shape-shifter whale-wolf creature, Akhlut, or a supernatural white wolf that transforms into the orca after entering the ocean, known by the wolf's tracks to and from the water. White wolves are ascribed supernatural powers. There is another Inuit story about Qisaruatsiaq, an abandoned old woman forced to survive on her own, which she does by turning into a wolf.

The Haida of British Columbia tell of a man living by the ocean who had two pet wolves that would hunt whales for him. They hunted more than the man could use, and the carcasses began to pile up. The Creator, seeing this waste, punished the two wolves by turning them into sea creatures— sea wolves. They were the parents of all orcas.

The Algonquin peoples believe in the god Michaboo, who employed wolves in the disguise of dogs to return order to the earth after the flood. Various native legends speak of a great flood, similar to the Bible stories. In one, it is not an ark but four wolf cubs that survived by climbing to the peak of a high mountain. After the waters subsided, the wolves howled, calling out for other survivors. Humans had also survived— perhaps they climbed to the peak of a different mountain! They heard the howls of the wolves and invited them into their community. Similarly, the creation story of the Kwakwaka'wakw of the Pacific Northwest explains that their nation descended from four wolves that, after the flood, shed their skins and became human. In a creation story of the Heiltsuck of the West Coast, a wolf fathers the first children:

one is born a wolf and serves as protector of the people, and the other children are born human and are the first Heiltsuck.

Coexistence of man and beast is a repeated theme in numerous human cultures and throughout recorded human history—a theme deep within the human psyche. There is considerable mythology and legend in cultures from around the world of humans adopted by wolves. The Wolf Mother in native mythology is sometimes depicted with a human child. There are stories, claiming to be non-fiction, of wolf children, orphans raised by wolves. In ancient Roman mythology, the most famous legend is probably that of Romulus and Remus, the twin sons of the god Mars who abandoned them as infants, fearing they would overthrow him when they were adults. Romulus and Remus were adopted and nursed by a she-wolf and grew up to rule the Roman Empire. Rudyard Kipling's *The Jungle Story* harked back to Romulus and Remus, with benevolent wolves adopting the human baby Mowgli and raising the man-cub as one of their own.

According to author Robert Lake-Thom, a Plains fable tells of a deceitful wife trying to seduce her husband's brother. When the brother refused her advances, she set up a pit-trap in the woods that he fell into and was left to perish. A group of wolves rescued him and adopted him into the pack; the young man accepted out of loyalty for saving his life. He lived among the wolves for some time until men from his camp saw him running with the wolves. They chased him down on their horses and captured him to bring to the elders. The young man explained his vow of loyalty and that he was unable to return to the camp unless the wolves granted him permission. His people released him to go and talk to his wolf family, after which he returned to camp with an offer. The wolf elders requested a deal in return for their son. The native people would be required to never kill a wolf without just cause and proper prayer payment. In return, the wolves would always bring special messages to the people, teach them to be skilled hunters and how to find game.

The Plains bands spoke of the wolf-helpers who guided, protected and fed lost or outcast people through strange lands. Leading warriors and chiefs often took wolf names. The Cherokee would not kill wolves. They believed that the brothers of the slain wolf would come for revenge, and that the weapon used to kill the wolf would not work again unless exorcised by a medicine man. The Ahtna people of the boreal forest felt that it was disrespectful to refer to certain animals by name; they called the wolf "takes-long-steps." They believed that showing the wolf this respect would bring good fortune and prevent them from harm. The wolf is present in many of the songs of the native peoples of the boreal forest.

Some tribes have wolf clans or societies. Wolf is a principal totem, crest animal or clan emblem of over 30 native families of the Pacific Northwest and over 30 nations of Huron. The Nootka of the Pacific Northwest have close spiritual ties with the wolf. The Tlingit have moieties, a lineage reference that divides down to smaller levels of family organization, and one of the two moieties is the wolf moiety. The wolf is also an alternative to the eagle as the crest of one of the two main Tlignit clans. Instead of having moieities, the Gitksan, Nisga'a and Tsimshian nations organize their societies into four clans or phratry, also known as *pteex*: the Laxsgiik (Eagle Clan), Gispwudwada (Killerwhale Clan), Ganhada (Raven Clan) and Laxgibuu (Wolf Clan). Laxgibuu derives from *gibuu*, which means "wolf" in the Gitksan and Nisga'a languages; the Tsimshian word for wolf is *gibaaw*, but they still use *Laxgibuu* for the wolf clan. Wolf Clan is a prominent clan in Anishinaabe (which includes the Algonquin, Ojibwa, Odawa and Potawatomi), Cree and Iroquoian groups in Ontario.

The wolf is celebrated by bands of the Northwest Territories in a masked festival called the Klukwalle or Klukwana Wolf Ritual. The wolf den and wolf bathhouse appear in crests of northern clans, which adorn clothing, homes, shields, drums and more. Whether it was superstition or perhaps fashion, images of the wolf are common on garments and other objects.

The Pawnee, Hidatsa and Otoe had wolf skin pouches to hold ceremonial amulets and important objects. Wolf skin was also considered to have powers or at least offer a bit of luck. One crest myth tells of an ancestral clan member who aided a wolf by removing a bone from the wolf's teeth. The man then became lucky and the clan adopted the wolf as its crest. The Assiniboine wore white wolf skin caps into battle for luck. Cheyenne medicine men rubbed wolf fur on arrows for good luck in the hunt. Cheyenne warriors were known as wolf soldiers and were made holy by rituals featuring dancers in wolf dress. Hidatsa women rubbed their stomachs with wolf skin to prevent or ease difficult childbirths. Plains groups, such as the Cree, had wolf dancers who transcended through dance to invoke the spirit of the wolf, one of their most important animal spirits. Medicine men of BC's Kwakwaka'wakw peoples wore wolf robes.

With the glory of the wolf living on, alongside the preservation of its habitat, "everything will be good," as the Cheyenne scout says. The wolf will continue to inspire and intrigue. Through perseverance and strength, it will convince man of its worth and in doing so will save all the humble creatures sharing its domain, and perhaps bring man's salvation as well, the humblest creature of all. Native peoples today still view the wolf as a brother sharing the struggle and experience of a native survivor.

The native peoples of North America saw the beasts of the wilderness as kin. They never vilified any animal; instead, they sanctified them. It's not that they didn't hunt wolves—they hunted many species of animal, but on a need basis, never with hatred and never to exterminate. How different would the perspective be in the next wave of human migration to the New World.

EUROPEANS

Europeans came onto the scene with a very different paradigm than the imagined utopian existence of the native peoples living alongside the wolf as a brother. The first Europeans came in the 1500s; they were the whalers, fishermen, explorers and trappers of New France. Settling the country began as French and English colonies were established in the 17th century. These Europeans brought with them their prejudices about wolves, many from the old European folklore rather than from actual experience or encounters. The wolf has often been a metaphor for evil. Just a few examples are the werewolves of Europe, the mythical Teutonic wolf who devours the sun and the Big Bad Wolf in children's stories. The fear of wolves brought on their relentless persecution, driven by violence and hatred.

Europeans considered wolves to be monsters, brutal and bloodthirsty, feared and vilified and hunted with a vengeance. Ideologically, the wolf was a symbol of what was wild and untamed, contrary to the settlers' ideal of civilization and control. Practically, the wolf was a hindrance to early settlers who had to hunt to survive. They saw the wolf as competition, and if they had livestock, wolves were perceived as a risk for livestock depredation. Today we praise the wildness of the wolf, yearning for something we are losing as we find ourselves more separated from the wild, but the same attribute was negative to the early settlers. Wilderness was contrary to their ideal of civilization and control, and the wolf represented what was impeding the achievement of this goal. The early settlers were in the wild but wanted to be in the safety of politely groomed civilization.

Wolves in Literature

At my little country school where almost all of my classmates lived on acreages and farms, we had a lot of practical application for what were taught in our natural science classes. We could relate to a lot of the literature that is standard curriculum for young people, often about animals and typically tragic—like Frederick Benjamin Gipson's *Old Yeller* and John Steinbeck's *The Red Pony*. These American novels spoke of the cruelties of nature we were already familiar with, but also of the joy in bonding with animals. It wasn't much of a leap to see these themes emerge in Canadian literature, but with relationships applying to wild animals. Canadian authors gave voice to a shy Canadian perspective that appreciated nature, and in some way gave voice to the animals themselves.

A new genre of Canadian literature became popular in the mid-19th century, portraying life of the immigrant or colonial people in a new country. This was widely appealing and fashionable in Britain, where most of Canada's first wave of immigration came from. The stories were about the challenges of a new landscape and first impressions and encounters with native peoples and wild animals.

Back in Britain, a persistent view of the animal world had been strongly inclined toward the pastoral comforts of domestic life, with cute little ducks and bunnies. Beatrix Potter's *Peter Rabbit* and *The Tale of Jemima Puddle-Duck* contended with the villainous fox, wolf and weasel, while Kenneth Grahame's poor mole got lost in the woods as dusk falls, which is apparently unnerving for a near-blind nocturnal animal, in the slightly scary *The Wind in the Willows*. The Brits desired the safe and cozy world connected to the hearth. But the Brits who came to North America could no longer relate to that world. Their new world had a wildness about it. But they also recognized, for the first time perhaps, the fragility of this seemingly hostile world. Through Canadian literature about wildlife and wilderness, British immigrants recovered a sense of salvation from the decimation of the land that had occurred in Europe at the wills and ignorance of their forebears.

Writings about wild animals strongly identified the Canadian persona. The "animal story" was the first distinctively Canadian genre. Author Ernest Thompson Seton (1860–1946), self-christened Black Wolf, was one of the founders of this Canadian art form. It was Seton's work *Wild Animals I Have Known* (1898) that set the stage for the true animal story genre. In this book is "Lobo, the King of Currumpaw," the tragic true story of Seton being among the men who hunted down two wolves for killing livestock, and how the vengeful, inhumane hunt and the dignity of the wolves changed his views of wildlife forever. He became an advocate for their protection and respect. Seton's revelation resonated with generations of naturalists throughout North America and in Britain, including David Attenborough, who attests that Seton was an inspiration for his remarkable career. The story of Lobo was made into a Disney film in 1962. Seton influenced his fellow Canadian writers, thus launching the animal story genre.

Ever since Lobo, my sincerest wish has been to impress upon people that each of our native wild creatures is in itself a precious heritage that we have no right to destroy or put beyond the reach of our children.

–Ernest Thompson Seton

Seton was born in England but immigrated to Canada in 1866 with his parents when he was a young boy. He spent his boyhood years in rural Ontario and Manitoba; according to his biography, it was running around in the woods and "playing Indian" that influenced his life as a writer and naturalist. I really don't know if kids still do this today, but playing Cowboys and Indians, riding horses and imagining living in the wilderness with wild animal companions surely has been an imaginative pastime for generations of Canadian kids. The life of the native peoples in pre-colonial times is immensely appealing to children—and many adults as well! It was a romanticized, naïve and archaic view, but Seton wrote about this paradigm in his book *Two Little Savages; Being the Adventures of Two Boys Who Lived as Indians and What They Learned* (1906).

Seton's earlier writings on wild animals inspired Sir Charles G.D. Roberts (1860–1943), who wrote *Kindred of the*

Wild (1902) and *Red Fox* (1905), among a long list of titles and collections of short stories, mainly about animals. Roberts' writing drew upon his childhood experiences in the wilderness of the Maritimes.

Robert William Service (1874–1958) left Scotland for Canada at age 21 to work at the Canadian Bank of Commerce in the Yukon. There he fell in love with Canadian wilderness and found his calling as poet and writer; that love affair with the North has left him with epitaphs such as the "Canadian Kipling" and "Bard of the Yukon."

On the ragged edge of the world I'll roam.
And the home of the wolf shall be my home.

–Robert Service, "Nostomaniac," *Rhymes of a Rolling Stone* (1912)

Jack London (1876–1916), although American, was also captivated by the Canadian wilderness of the North and wrote about adventures set in the gold rush era of the Yukon in his short story collection *The Son of the Wolf* (1900) and novels *Call of the Wild* (1903) and *White Fang* (1906). *White Fang* is about a three-quarters wolf/one-quarter dog hybrid that starts life as an Inuit sled dog, but later is sold as a fighting dog until a kind man tries to tame him again. *Call of the Wild* is the author's most famous work, grappling with the divide between wolf and dog: the wolf made gentle and the dog answering the call to return to the wild pack.

Canadians were also influenced by people who actualized a calling to embrace the native culture. There is no better example than the life story of Grey Owl (Wa-sha-quon-asin); he spoke with one of the most charismatic voices for the Canadian wilderness and its inhabitants in the 20th century. Born Archibald Belaney (1888–1938), he emigrated from England in 1906 on the SS *Canada* to Halifax, but reinvented himself soon after his arrival. Belaney discarded his English name and way of life, was adopted into the culture of the

Ojibwa peoples of Ontario, married an Ojibwa woman in 1910 and lived a humble and modest life in the woods at his cabin, Beaver Lodge. Rather than living his life in quiet seclusion, however, he reached out and shared it. He used the media, making films and writing books about his way of life and the animals he advocated for—particularly the iconic Canadian beaver. He reared two orphaned beavers left behind by the trappers who took their parents; the baby beavers were adorable and easily pulled on people's heartstrings. These beavers helped lead to trapping restrictions that saved the species from the overharvesting taking place at the time. Grey Owl captured imaginations, reminding Canadians of the connection they already had with nature: that our heritage with our native land was as poignant, if not more so, than the Old World our immigrant forefathers had left behind.

Mid- to late 20th-century Canadian literature dealt with native culture and the romance of a time quickly passing and a way of life quickly changing. J.F. Hayes wrote *Buckskin Colonist* (1947); Roderick Haig-Brown wrote about the Salish in *The Whale People* (1962); Cliff Faulknor wrote about the prairies during European colonialism in *The White Calf* (1965), *The White Peril* (1966) and *The Smoke Horse* (1968); and Doris Anderson wrote *Blood Brothers* (1967). Jan Hudson wrote *Sweetgrass* (1984) about a Blackfoot woman in the early 19th century, and Kevin Major wrote *Blood Red Ochre* (1989) about a native girl in Newfoundland and her Beothuk ancestry—the culture that went extinct alongside the Beothuk wolf. The native way of life, though compromised, was undeniably deeply within the Canadian psyche, and either felt like a guilty sin or a mourning of a perceived loss of innocence or youth. By making the same mistakes as other nations throughout other times, there was a lost chance to have become something different.

R.D. Lawrence, another Canadian wildlife writer, was a naturalist at heart and a field biologist by training, but a story-teller by calling, writing over 30 books, several in honour of the wolf: *Cry Wild* (1970), *Secret Go the Wolves* (1980), *In Praise of Wolves* (1986), *Wolves* (1990) and *Trail of the Wolf* (1993). R.D. Lawrence inspired and influenced establishment of the Wolf Centre at the Haliburton Forest in Ontario.

Probably the most famous Canadian wolf writer is the great Farley Mowat. Born in Ontario in 1921, he is one of the most prolific and widely read Canadian authors. His iconic book *Never Cry Wolf* (1963) was a pivotal piece of literature that is considered by many people to have forever changed a lingering negative public perception of wolves as vicious and bloodthirsty.

We have doomed the Wolf not for what it is, but for what we have deliberately and mistakenly perceived it to be... the mythologized epitome of a savage, ruthless killer, which is, in reality, no more than a reflexed image of ourself.

–Farley Mowat, *Never Cry Wolf*

At what point did non-native Canadians drop Old World perspectives of wolves and relate much more readily to the native perspective celebrating the wild, clawed and fanged animals? At what point did we as a nation recognize wilderness as part of our Canadian identity? Today, native ideology is integral to the Canadian identity, as was seen in the opening and closing ceremonies of the 2010 Olympic Winter Games. We acknowledge our British and French heritage and how it evolved to be something distinctly Canadian, but there were totem poles at the Olympic ceremonies, not Union Jacks. Perhaps we have come to not only respect but also share native perspectives about wildlife. But it has taken a while to get here...

THE FUR TRADE IN COLONIAL TIMES

Animal hides have always been a resource for humans for clothing and other textiles, and many other parts of the animal were used for various purposes. Native groups traded amongst each other, but for the most part had no conflicts until times of shortage—which happened once the Europeans increased the demand for fur beyond the sustained use by local inhabitants to feed the demands of fashion-hungry populations an ocean away. Native peoples were subsistent and bartered for what they needed—and they had had all they needed. There was trade of necessary provisions such as meat, skins and plants between groups, and non-essential goods such as tobacco, beads and tools were traded openly and communally, often as gifts. This suited the Europeans when they were on the receiving end, but when reciprocity was demanded, the Europeans viewed the native peoples as beggars and thieves. Europeans brought with them novelties and practical goods that had never been seen before by the native peoples. When they saw what the Europeans had, they began trading for the new and interesting articles in exchange for the European's limitless desire for furs, which created an incentive for the native hunters to overharvest.

After guns and ammunition were introduced, along with alcohol, iron tools, paint and beads, the demand for those new items was limitless. The only form of currency to purchase the items was in beaver pelts, grizzly bear and buffalo robes, wolf skins and horses, which had a limit in nature but no limit of demand in Europe. The introduction of guns into the native culture disrupted a sensitive balance of power. Territories had been established and respected between native groups based upon group size, type of subsistence (whether they were nomadic hunters, pastoralists, fishers, etc.), alliances and attributes such as possession of horses. This all came unravelled when smaller groups obtained guns and could attack neighbouring groups. The price for purchasing guns was in pelts. The native peoples began hunting and trapping to exploitative levels. When their territories were exhausted they invaded neighbouring groups. Wars between native groups and the tension between natives and Europeans escalated to epic proportions. The native peoples' way of life was effectively destroyed, and the toll on wildlife was immense.

International marketing for Canada's fur, its premier resource, began early. The Hudson's Bay Company was established in 1670 and began operating from posts, or forts, along the coast of the Hudson Bay under a charter granted by the British crown. The company had a monopoly over all fur-trading territory in British North America. The fur traders and trappers were the first to explore the Canadian wilderness and establish contact with the native communities. The fur trade started at Hudson Bay and up the St. Lawrence to Montreal, the two main marine routes from Europe. Quebec has the oldest forts and longest history of the fur trade. The French and the British began vying to establish forts and control trade, and they started moving west in their quest for furs. The Seven Years' War (1756–63) between the French and English that led to the conquest of New France by Great Britain was also the time of the Great Indian War: native peoples were manipulated in the colonial conquests between the French and British who allied with various groups and pitted them against each other in trade. (Incidentally, it was General James Wolfe who won Quebec for Britain on the Plains of Abraham in 1759.)

One of the most exemplary situations depicting this manipulation of the native peoples during colonization is the plight of the Atsinas, most commonly referred to as the Gros Ventre, the name given to them by the Europeans. The Gros Ventre were nomadic buffalo hunters and the most powerful band of Canada's Great Plains, in part because of their possession of horses. They began to trade furs, mainly wolf skins and buffalo robes, to the Europeans primarily for brandy and guns, which were now in the hands of other bands

Fur pelts for sale in Calgary, Alberta, 1922.

and threatened the position of the Gros Ventre in the balance of power on the prairies. The Gros Ventre had occupied Manitoba's parkland belt but were expelled in the early 1700s by the Cree and Assiniboine after these two bands acquired guns from French *coureurs de bois* (unlicensed fur traders) in exchange for furs. The Cree and Assiniboine had over-trapped their own mammal base to feed the endless demand of the Europeans for furs to ship abroad. They invaded the Gros Ventre territory in search of more beaver.

The Gros Ventre migrated west to the Saskatchewan prairies and formed alliances with the Blackfoot, Blood and Peigan, who shared the same Algonquian language base and had formed the Blackfoot Confederacy. Next the Tsuu T'ina also joined, although they were Athapaskan-speaking, and this alliance dominated the western prairies of Canada until the Cree and Assiniboine invaded west again. They massacred an entire Gros Ventre band in 1793, causing the Gros Ventre to split into two groups and abandon their hunting grounds again. One group retreated to the Missouri with the Arapaho, to whom they are related, and the second moved farther southwest along the South Saskatchewan River and around the Cypress Hills. After 1831, even this group moved south across the American border, and the Cree and Assiniboine took over the entire Canadian prairies and allied with the Hudson's Bay Company, claiming it over the French forts in the west. Throughout this migration of the native peoples, European voyageurs followed the native travel routes through the Rockies in search of furs. Eventually, the Canadian Pacific Railway opened the West to settlement.

Joseph F. Dion, in *My Tribe the Crees*, says, "As the white man began to make inroads into our stamping grounds, bringing with him new and wicked weapons, he set to work to destroy everything wherever he went. Buffalo hides and furs were bringing in a fair price so he wantonly shot down thousands of our noble animals, stripped off the hides and left tons of good meat to rot on the prairies. Some of these independent hunters with a view to easily obtaining a few wolf pelts deliberately set poison at random, thereby killing immense numbers of flesh-eating animals and birds. This utter disregard for natural law coupled with the white man's diseases and his plain cruel selfishness created for the proud, easygoing Plains Cree, a period of untold misery and brought about their ultimate degradation."

The Economics of the Fur Trade

Beaver pelts launched the fur trade in Canada, which is why, almost like an apology, the beaver became the national emblem after it was almost hunted to extinction—much like the grizzly bear is the emblem of the state of California, where the species is now extirpated.

Beaver

The wool layer close to the skin of the beaver could be processed to a fine felt. It became the material for making hats throughout Europe as well as in Canada and the United States. Nearly every hat from 1600–1800 that you see in photos and in museums is likely made from felt from Canadian beavers. Ladies and men, commoners and gentry and even cardinals and popes wore hats made from beaver.

In the 17th and 18th centuries, beaver was the highest-valued fur and set the standard, like currency or gold, for the value of all other furs matched against it. Red fox, black bear, muskrat, otter and wolf were important furs and were valued against a single beaver pelt. For example, a wolf or red fox pelt was of equal value to one beaver; two otter or six muskrat were valued at one beaver; one black bear was worth five beavers. They were valued against the beaver to encourage the native trappers to bring in more of the desired furs to trade. The native peoples would bring in the pelts of animals they never traditionally hunted, strange undesirable pelts such as skunk or muskrat. Rocky Mountain House was one fort where every mammal was trapped and traded.

For transport, furs were packed and pressed into bales, with a typical bale consisting of 10 buffalo robes, or 45 wolf pelts, or 100 fox, or 70 beaver, with a couple dozen badger for good measure. At the height of fur bartering, the Canadian fur trade shipped 300,000 beaver pelts, 50,000 bear pelts and 30,000 wolf pelts back to Europe each year.

The Canadian fur trade endured its first economic crash in the 1830s and '40s, when the beaver felt hat that had been in vogue in Europe for more than 200 years was no longer in fashion. The style for hats turned to silk, which was more lightweight and cooler in the summer. The Hudson's Bay Company was unable to sell its stockpiles of beaver pelt to the London market. In the mid-19th century, buffalo and marten became the highest pelts of demand. In 1810–11, three buffalo were slightly less than one prime beaver, and pre-1840s, one marten was about half a prime beaver. However, in the 1850s and '60s, one buffalo was almost equal to one and a half prime beaver, and one marten was worth two prime beaver. In other words, buffalo and marten had quadrupled in value as compared to beaver.

The slowly but steadily lowering fur demand from European markets coinciding with fewer people living traditional hunting and trapping lifestyles likely saved many species from near or total extinction. In the 1990s, the Hudson's Bay Company closed the fur component of its business. (For more about the fur trade today, see The Modern Fur Trade in Canada, p. 145.)

BOUNTIES

A draft of such a well-known animal is useless. Described in all the accounts are its dog-like shape with pointed muzzle, a colour of yellow-tan and its long and bulky tail. It has a worker's physique. It's a gangster and has the air of one...It's extremely slim, more defiant

than its cousin the fox and his follower-in-mischief the
wolverine. To catch a glimpse of the animal in the forest
is not easy. The acuity of its sense of smell is incredible;
it will hunt you out at any distance. Defiant to the
utmost, surprisingly cunning and amazing cowards
when they are alone, they become insolent, aggressive
and dangerous when reunited in a group...Despite the
beauty of its fur, there is no question in rearing
a scourge of this kind. The wolf must be destroyed...

–Henride Puvialon, Quebec naturalist (1900)

The use of wolves for their pelts went from a traditional subsistence harvest to a commercial demand for fashion. Even when the demand for its fur began to wane, the wolf remained of value in the form of bounty reward. The public paradigm toward wolves became one that predominantly sought the eradication of wolves in Canada, similar to in the United States. Many Canadians today would agree that one of the defining elements of Canada is its wildlife and wild spaces, but in 1867, the year Canada was born as a nation, many Canadians saw the wolf as something to be exterminated and the wilds that it lived in to be tamed. In medieval times, wolves were not just hunted, but they were tortured, often burned at the stake like witches. We regard these actions with disgust, yet within the last 100 years, documentation reminds us that North American wolves were burned alive, dragged behind horses and mutilated, and captured only to have their lower jaws cut off and turned free to starve. The intent to exterminate wolves from Canada was a goal as recent as the 1960s—and the central prairies and the Maritimes succeeded. Still today in North America, wolves are shot, trapped and poisoned, primarily to limit their numbers.

The United States was colonized much earlier than Canada, and wolf bounties were in place in New England as early as 1630. By 1900, wolves were rare or absent from all of eastern United States. The 1960s saw the final demise of the wolf in the lower 48 states. The only remaining wolves were in extreme northeastern Minnesota (350–700) and on Isle Royale (only about 20). By 1965, the eastern timber wolf was thought to occur in only 3% of its former range in the US outside of Alaska.

It was 1793 that marked the inglorious year that Canada held its first wolf bounty, in Ontario and Quebec, then known as Upper and Lower Canada. Upper Canada (southern Ontario) and Lower Canada (Quebec and Labrador) were deemed the original provinces of the British Colony on December 26, 1791. Nova Scotia and New Brunswick were the next two British colonies (established February 10, 1841); these two colonies along with the two provinces of Upper and Lower Canada, became a federation of four provinces on July 1, 1867. In true colonial fashion, the European founders of Canada began to kick out several of the existing tenants of the land. Extirpation of the wolf from eastern Canada was imminent by the 1870s: the wolf was extirpated from New Brunswick by 1880 and from Nova Scotia by 1900. In Newfoundland (which did not become a Canadian province until 1949) the wolf was officially declared extinct in 1930, though the last one reported was seen and shot in 1913. Aggressive predator-control and predator-eradication pro-grams and the plummeting populations of prey species such as caribou and beaver resulted in the eradication of the wolf from the Maritimes. Historical records of the price paid for wolf bounties in this era are scant, but were less than or up to $1 per wolf.

The West began establishing wolf bounties in the 1800s. Wolf numbers in the prairies and eastern Canada began dwindling owing to the demise of bison as well as elk, moose and other deer species in the 1860s and 1870s during European settlement and agricultural development.

The anti-wolf sentiment spread north. In the Northwest Territories, a wolf control program was put in place to increase ungulate populations for human consumption. In 1924–33, a $30 bounty and mass wolf poisoning campaign went alongside the continued hunting of barren-ground caribou on Southampton Island. Allegedly, 1000 wolves were killed per year while human hunting of caribou continued. By 1950, both animals were extinct. In 1967, caribou were reintroduced to Southampton Island, and with no natural predators, the population boomed and is now overgrazing the island. In general, from the 1900s onward, wolf bounties have ranged in price from $10–$50 per pelt.

Strychnine was used to poison wolves in the Yukon in the 1920s, and bounties were introduced in the '30s. It is estimated that about 500 wolves per year were killed during these decades. West of the Rockies, things were much the same. British Columbia instigated its first wolf bounty in the late 1870s. When bounties were not sufficiently effective, the government established a predator control division in 1947 to systematically cull wolves with the use of several types of poison.

Not even the national parks were safe for wolves. Ironically, it was during the 19th century when this attack on nature was taking place that Canada's first national park was established: Banff National Park was inaugurated in 1885. Alberta extended the existing wolf bounty throughout the province, including within the national parks. The last wolves were extirpated from Waterton Lakes National Park in 1922 and from Banff National Park by 1930. Wolves were controlled in the national parks throughout the 1940s and '50s, owing to concern for ungulate herds. And yet generations of park wardens and provincial biologists spent their entire careers managing elk, deer, sheep, goats, moose...all the main ungulate prey species in the absence of their main predator, the wolf. Even Dewey Soper, one of Canada's eminent biologists and naturalists, pushed for wolf control.

[T]here dead wolves are better than none and the three dead, incontestably dead. They are beyond the powers of reproduction and destruction. If we want to kill wolves, does it much matter, within reason, how they become defunct? The point as I see it under the circumstances is to momentarily set aside some of the disputations of the situation and go straight to the objective—reduction of the wolf population. The answer is comparatively simple—"kill them."

–Dewey Soper, biologist and naturalist

Predator-control programs in the recent past have been advocated for and sometimes instigated by an aggressive vocal minority, but time has shown that the majority of Canadians are tolerant and appreciative of wolves. Sadly, it only takes one visibly or vocally intolerant rancher to give all ranchers that same reputation. In the United States, where wolf reintroduction is underway, one intolerant person with a rifle can undermine years of work and funding, despite an acceptance of wolves by the majority of people in the area.

Case Study: Bounties in Alberta

The first wolf bounty in Alberta was not launched by the provincial government's wildlife department; the public disapproved of such heavy-handed, bloody programs. Established in the southern prairies in 1899, the first Alberta wolf bounty was administered by the Western Stock Growers' Association. They funded and paid for the tails of approximately 2850 individual wolves in a mere seven-year period (the bounty stopped paying out in 1907). The wolf was under no form of species protection or bag limit as a controlled game species, so this minority association was able to purchase the eradication of wolves from the agricultural prairie belt. In

1909, the provincial legislature assented to "An Act for the Payment of Wolf Bounty," paying $10 per timber wolf, $1 per coyote and $1 per wolf pup. This fee was amended in 1917 to increase the payment for female timber wolves to $20 and then amended again in 1927 to increase the bounty payment for pups to $2. In 1931, payments for wolf bounties were discontinued by Order in Council, but the stoppage was short-lived: four years later the bounty was reinstated. In 1937 the payments were reduced to $5 for all adult wolves (the payment for pups remained at $2), but the next year, the payment went back up to $10 for adults and $5 for pups. In 1942, special snaring permits were issued to trappers to assist in wolf capture, and payments for any wolf, male or female, adult or pup, were $10 across the board by 1943. Neck snares were allowed on registered traplines in 1945, and that year the bounty took a sharp leap to a whopping $25 per wolf during a specified hunting season (April 1 to October 15).

Full-scale eradication programs in the central provinces peaked in the 1950s. By then, wolves were almost completely eliminated from the Alberta prairies. In the early 1950s, snaring of wolves was legalized and cyanide "coyote-getters" were distributed to forestry personnel. The cyanide was targeted at coyotes, but of course would have poisoned wolves, foxes and any other hapless scavengers that happened to come across the bait. Alberta Fish and Wildlife staff used the same coyote-getters to actively reduce wolf and coyote numbers in forested areas throughout the province in the 1950s, and soon after, strychnine baits were used by the game commission in the Clearwater Forest to reduce wolf predation to secure populations of game animals for hunting.

Then, to make a dire situation worse, the 1952 breakout of rabies in foxes and coyotes justified a heavy-handed poisoning campaign that lasted four years, killing thousands of wolves—the disease was discovered in only a single wolf. Not only wolves were poisoned under this hysteria, but so were count-less thousands of additional animals—foxes, coyotes, hawks, eagles, owls, ravens, magpies, mustelids, lynx, bobcats. This massive impact was considered acceptable because these species were perceived as threats to game and livestock or simply as unimportant or nuisance animals. John Stelfox, wildlife manager in the province at the time, estimated that only 500–1000 wolves survived in all of Alberta. The use of toxicants continued until the mid-1960s to counter game herd and livestock predation and enhance hunting opportunities. Competition with game hunters and ranchers was used as justification for the wolf's virtual eradication. Bounties were placed upon wolves to allow continued hunting on threatened game populations.

Bounties Across Canada

Eternal truths that shame our soothing lies.

—Robert Service

Alberta is an easy case study for an embarrassing example of a wolf-eradication program, but much of the country was doing the same thing. The beginning of the end of government-imposed bounties was in 1954, when the Canadian Predator Control Conference was held in Calgary. The abandonment of bounties was strongly recommended. In 1955, the BC Game Commission abandoned its bounty system, becoming the first wildlife agency in North America to do so. It took over 20 years for bounties to be discontinued throughout the provincial and territorial level in Canada.

When Quebec announced a wolf kill contest in the winter of 1971–72, encouraging hunters to shoot wolves ($50 per pelt, $25 per head, with the first 50 hunters to bring in a wolf carcass to Tourism, Fish and Game promised a trophy of the wolf's lower jaw encased in plastic with the hunter's name on a plaque), there was some significant public outcry heard throughout the country. The bounty was soon revoked.

Certain municipalities in Quebec have occasionally offered bounties, but wolves are managed on a provincial level with controlled hunting and trapping seasons.

In November 1972, the Ontario government repealed its wolf bounty established in 1793.

Wolf bounties had become so controversial in Canada that in February 1973, a joint agreement between Canada and the United States for a moratorium on wolf hunting was proposed. The bill was proposed by the Jethro Wildlife Fund. Jethro was the name of a captive wolf owned by John Harris of the North American Association for the Preservation of Predatory Animals. Harris took Jethro, a 40 kg, 7-year-old male Canadian grey/timber wolf, and Clem, a 50 kg, 4-year-old female Alaskan wolf, on a tour of Canada in 1973, visiting schools where children were able to pet the tame wolves. The lengthy tour aspired to increase public awareness about wolves and increase support, advocacy and tolerance of wild predatory animals. At the completion of the tour, the team stopped for the night in Brooklyn on their route home. During the night, a person snuck into the compound where the wolves were being kept in a pen and fed them strychnine-laced chicken. Harris found the two wolves in the morning, dead in their enclosure. Though a bill on a hunting moratorium never came to pass, Harris's work did much for wolf conservation in North America at the time, such as influencing the US Endangered Species Act, and carries on today with the work of Mission:Wolf in Colorado, a wolf sanctuary and educational foundation.

In the Slave River lowlands in the Northwest Territories in 1977, a $300 bounty was placed on the wolf's head to allow continued bison hunting. The desire to continue bison hunting justified trapping and aerial shooting of wolves; within a couple of years the wolf population went from 72 to 2 individuals and the bison from 2100 to 600. The bounty was revoked in 1979, making the Northwest Territories the last provincial or territorial jurisdiction in Canada to abandon the bounty system.

The current policy of the Northwest Territories Department of Environment and Natural Resources is that no wolf control will be implemented unless it is clear that bison, muskoxen, moose or caribou populations are threatened "because of wolf predation." This policy is in conjunction with controls on hunting if hunting has been identified as a contributing factor to population declines.

In the 1980s in Alberta, a controversial wolf bounty was proposed by hunters and seriously considered by Fish and Wildlife, but was rejected as a result of negative public feedback. Then, much like the Western Stock Growers' Association of the first Alberta wolf bounty, the Alberta Trappers' Association proposed a $100 "trapping incentive" in 1989 on the first 50 wolves with an aim to remove 250 wolves per year. The intent was to reduce wolf numbers in west-central Alberta and restore woodland caribou and elk populations. Again, Albertans raised their voices in protest and the bounty was not implemented.

Even on a municipal level, the use of the word "bounty" is unacceptable throughout the country, but has been replaced by terms such as "incentive" or "compensation." One of the last true bounties was discontinued in the Yukon in 1991. Yet, one rural municipality in Saskatchewan was offering a reward of $100 per wolf at the time of writing this book, and the Clear Hills County in the Peace River region of Alberta implemented a Wolf Hunt Incentive Policy in July 2010 to pay $500 per adult wolf and $250 per non-adult wolf taken. These are just two examples, but throughout Canada various rural municipalities implement reward schemes to hunt or trap wolves. Wildlife agencies need to take responsibility for dealing with specific problem wolves rather than unintentionally create public vigilante-style wolf control. One only needs to read a trophy hunting blog to hear the excitement over bagging a wolf for monetary reward. There is something innately offensive that points to glaring inadequacy in natural resource management when reward schemes replace the implementation of scientifically backed environmental policies and hunters and trappers have to be bribed into overharvesting. Although the word "bounty" is in rare use, and placing monetary prizes on wolves' heads is shunned, wolves still today are wanted on reward.

THE GREEN MOVEMENT

Continuing with the momentum of the peace movement and protest to end the Vietnam War that started in the 1960s, the 1970s saw the birth of the tree-hugger and the beginning of a movement to end the war on nature. The first Earth Day was in June 1970, and the Sierra Club was established in Canada the same year. Green Peace, probably the most prominent and iconic environmental organization in the world, was established in Vancouver in 1971. The first acts to protect endangered species in Canada passed in Ontario in 1971; Canada's endangered species protection acts were the first in the world to seek protection of all rare or endangered plants and animals (including insects). The list of species at risk began to be defined in 1978 through the new intergovernmental COSEWIC. The scientific community had already found its public voice through the founding of the Canadian Wildlife Federation back in 1962, followed by the Canadian World Wildlife Fund (WWF) in 1967.

Douglas H. Pimlott (1920–78) is considered by many people to be the founder of the modern environmental movement in Canada. He was a renowned conservationist, wildlife biologist, ecologist and environmentalist and was one of the first stewards of the wolf and its conservation in Canada. He founded the Canadian Nature Federation while still a young man in 1939 (which in 2004 changed its name to Nature Canada), the Canadian Parks and Wilderness Society (1963), the Canadian Arctic Resources Committee (1971) and the World Conservation Union's Wolf Specialists Group (1973). Created over 30 years ago, the Douglas H. Pimlott Award is Nature Canada's pre-eminent award, given to the most influential Canadian naturalists and conservationists, including WWF Canada's President Emeritus Monte Hummel, who has also done much for wolf conservation. Much of Pimlott's pioneering work on wolves took place in Algonquin Provincial Park and in Alberta's mountain parks.

John Theberge was a student of Douglas Pimlott, and he continued to work with Algonquin wolves. John and his wife Mary researched the wolves in and around Algonquin Provincial Park for over a decade and are largely responsible for any protected status those wolves have been given. Their book *Wolf Country* is a must-read.

In the West, eminent and influential wolf conservationists emerged in Alberta's Rocky Mountains and into the foothills and northern boreal forests. Lu Carbyn was Pimlott's last student before he retired; Carbyn went on to become one of Canada's top pioneering wolf researchers. He worked in Jasper, as well as in Riding Mountain and Wood Buffalo National Parks. Carbyn was a biologist with the Canadian Wildlife Service in 1967 and a research scientist in 1974, and is currently the Canadian member of the International Union for the Conservation of Nature and Natural Resources (IUCN) Wolf Specialist Group and Canid Group. Paul Paquet implemented WWF's Southern Rockies Canine Project in Banff National Park. T.J. (Dick) Dekker worked in Jasper National Park. These individuals worked in the Rockies, one of the most densely human-inhabited wilderness areas of Canada, and can be credited for any science that was heeded (and likely a lot that was not heeded) in Alberta's recent history of wolf management. All have written numerous books, articles and research papers on wolves in Canada while being outspoken defenders of wolves and habitat conservation.

Notable American conservationists of Canadian wolves include David Mech, who has extensively studied several populations of Canadian wolves and added a library of information on our wolves, and wildlife photographer Jim Brandenburg, who added much of our awareness and most of the first photographs of the Canadian arctic wolves of Ellesmere Island.

One of the Vancouverites who founded Green Peace was Paul Watson, who later became an influential advocate for wolf conservation in Canada. After leaving Green Peace in the '80s, Watson formed his own anti-whaling organization, Sea Shepherd. While he was protesting the whaling in eastern Canada, the government confiscated his boat, and he found himself again in his home province of BC. While he was grounded, he learned about the aerial hunt underway by the government that was culling back the wolf population to increase game numbers. Watson was naturally opposed and a natural activist and so, in 1984, he founded Friends of the Wolf/Wolf Defence, "a conservation group devoted exclusively to the protection of wolves and wolf habitat." The group's aims were to halt the slaughter of the wolves in BC and fight the wolf's three main threats: government wolf-control programs, wolf bounties and the elimination of wolf habitat. They carried out non-violent direct action and raised public awareness about how wolves were being managed in the province and across the country.

Far from being a management program to deal with random problem wolves in agricultural areas, the culling in BC was a government-sanctioned eradication of wolves in lieu of habitat protection. Instead of the government working to solve the greater problem of habitat protection where wildlife population dynamics could be restored, wolves were being killed to silence vocal minorities, namely ranchers and hunters, who were against wolves. I met Paul Watson in the '90s when he came to give a lecture at my university on wolf conservation issues. He showed similar footage to that which had affected

me years before, but this time I was less shocked and more active. I recently met up with Watson again and asked him if he thought that things were improving for wolves in BC. He didn't think so, and was still amazed and disgusted that wolf culling (possibly incorporating costly aerial shooting by biologists working for the government) was ongoing instead of habitat protection. At the time of writing this book, the BC Ministry of Environment maintained that it is against current government policy to kill wolves from aircraft and that the only current direct government control program of wolves was in support of the Mountain Caribou Recovery Implementation Program.

Today in Canada there are countless organizations working in support of wildlife or wilderness conservation or preservation. They work to increase public education and awareness of ecology and nature. With the ever-increasing impacts of dirty petroleum-based energy, deforestation, climate change and unsustainable and ethically questionable agricultural practices and policies, there is urgent need for more advocacy and awareness for alternatives and solutions to these pressing issues. We need to ensure the survival of wilderness and natural systems and the health of all living things on our abused planet.

Current Wolf Management in Canada

They kill them on Vancouver Island because they're near deer. They kill them in the south because they don't want any wolves in their cattle. They kill them in the north because they eat moose. It's getting to the point where the wolf has nowhere to go.

–Jack Laufer, Director of the Northwest
Wildlife Preservation Society

In my opinion, it is not wildlife that needs to be managed, but human attitudes and actions, to establish hunting quotas and curb habitat destruction. Wildlife management is most often mitigating human activities that negatively affect wildlife areas. We admit to not understanding how most living things function in all their intricate, mysterious and interconnected ways, yet we are precocious enough to consider ourselves able to dictate or "manage" how other species exist.

Wild systems are to greater or lesser degrees managed throughout much of Canada, particularly in the parks and near human settlement. Priorities have often been to manage game species with high human value such as moose and deer, often with overinflated populations to ensure that hunters are content. As wildlife habitat continues to be fragmented or is completely removed by industry and development, increased human–wildlife conflict occurs. Predators, which were in the habitat before humans were, are then blamed for preying on pets or livestock, damaging what is now considered human property and occasionally coming in direct contact with people, which occasionally results in human injury. When habitat destruction occurs, the wildlife is managed not in relation to its biological-carrying capacity, which is a naturally occurring, self-regulating system, in which sustainable hunting and trapping can have a role, but in relation to the cultural-carrying capacity. The cultural capacity is wildlife population tolerance, which creates a labour-intensive, non-sustainable and artificial system. Rather than identifying sustainable quotas for hunting and trapping, incentives are put in place to overharvest to reduce wolf populations for our more often politically determined, rather than scientifically determined, wolf population targets. There is money to be made from high-paying American trophy hunters who come to Canada to shoot our biggest and most beautiful, possibly most genetically significant wolves, bears, cougars and other wildlife that they cannot shoot in the US, either because of hunting bans or because these species were already shot to extinction.

With more and more industrial bullying and wallet jangling, I look at many of the people who choose to work in service of nature—our park wardens, wildlife biologists, technicians and managers—with sympathy. I find that their expertise has little influence over policy implemented by governments who are puppeteered by private industry. My former professor and advisor during my undergrad in Wildlife and Conservation Biology at the University of Alberta shared with me his closing speech from the Second North American Symposium on Wolves in Edmonton in 1992. He couldn't have expressed this sentiment better when he said:

"How honourable it is to have a life dedicated to being in service...with all the dedication, patience, hard work, study, non-thanks…[to] protect and save wolves, not for the public. Not really, although there are public benefits we can cite. We save wolves—for their own sake—their own intrinsic right to exist…We eventually come to see them as our client. Many of you may still see your agency or your institution or the public at large as your client. Your client is that which commands your allegiance; that whom you act in the best interest for. You need ask at all decision points concerning the wolf, "Is this in the best interest of my client?" The other test is simply to ask yourself if the wolf had the opportunity to vote on your re-election as its representative, would it re-elect you? Would it really choose you? If you truly believe that to be so, then you are truly in service. And you command respect; and the eagles will bow and the wolves will howl to you."

CULLING

There are two factors to consider in the ongoing practice of culling wolves: one is pragmatic and ecological, the other touches on ethics. Given the complexity of predator–prey relationships within a larger paradigm that includes other prey species and habitat parameters, it is questionable whether wolf culling really makes any difference to a meagre herd. While wolves make a huge impact on prey numbers and are definitely a threat to a severely endangered prey species, culling is not likely effective on its own. Killing pack members may cause the remaining wolves with handicapped hunting abilities to take down smaller susceptible prey such as a caribou or a caribou calf rather than an elk or a moose in that same habitat. There is also the likelihood that another wolf pack or lone wolves would simply move into the territory of the compromised or exterminated pack. Another important question is how the caribou population become so low in the first place. The answer is not from wolves over-hunting caribou—it is from humans destroying caribou habitat and over-hunting them as a game species back when their numbers were stronger. Is it ethical to target wolves as the scapegoat for the plight of the caribou when habitat protection is the key to saving the species?

Jim Pissot, the executive director of the Canmore-based Defenders of Wildlife Canada, calls wolf culls "barroom biology," referencing the 217 wolves shot or poisoned near caribou herds over three winters from 2005 to 2008. "Albertans care about wolves, grizzlies, wilderness and the pace of unplanned development," said Pissot. "Perhaps the province is beginning to realize that a caribou 'recovery plan' that poisons wolves—while encouraging roads, developments and other habitat destruction in critical habitat—is nothing but a fraud and a hoax."

When habitat is fragmented, ungulate populations can become disassociated with predator populations (as occurs with elk in Banff) or more closely associated with predators that they could previously avoid (as with caribou in the Alberta foothills). When wolves are overpopulated in relation to a prey base, or change their prey preference because of opportunities that humans mistakably created (e.g., habitat alteration or placing cattle in proximity to forest fringe habitat), the short-term solution is to cull wolf numbers. We, the Canadian public, then stand by embarrassed by international and scientific scrutiny. When we hear in the news about wolf culls, it is not that there are too many wolves, it is that there are more wolves in certain areas than humans are willing to tolerate, or too many in comparison to demised prey species' populations—owing to human errors in wildlife and wildlife habitat management. That wolves are the threat to ungulates with unsustainably low populations is controversial. What caused the ungulate population declines and what, besides wolf culling, is being done to remedy the problem to restore threatened ungulate populations back to sustainable levels?

There are many reasons for reduced ungulate populations besides wolf predation and hunting. There is sometimes unmonitored aboriginal harvest (leaving guesswork for remaining numbers for commercial harvest), habitat loss, harsh winters and snow conditions, disease, poaching and road kill. Yet hunting moratoriums are rare because wildlife management is largely funded by hunters and trappers. According to personal communication with the Ministère de l'Environnement et de la Faune, in Quebec, "controversy about wolf numbers arise only when the white-tailed deer population is declining after a couple of harsh winters. When winters are mild and the deer population maintains itself at a very high level, hunting success is quite high and everybody is happy." Recognition of wildlife conservation has established protected areas, hunting quotas and seasons and related species studies and management plans. However, a natural balance is rare, and our methods for restoring balance rarely rely upon our own sacrifices but on a continued toll on predator populations.

Almost all prey species of wolves that are now categorized as at risk, vulnerable or endangered did not become so by wolf predation, primarily or initially. Sometimes seasonal weather anomalies can devastate ungulate populations, as has been seen in the arctic with melting and freezing cycles that then cover vegetation with impenetrable ice layers, causing caribou to starve. Some fingers have pointed to climate change, again human-caused habitat alteration. More obviously, most habitat loss is from industrial development. This in combination with over-hunting can be enough to handicap prey populations from withstanding the impacts of their natural predators. Hunters sometimes accept not hunting—but not always. We have to realize that if we have to keep killing wolves, we are probably not doing enough about habitat protection. Culling wolves is a temporary, quick fix to ease pressure on vulnerable prey species, but not a long-term sustainable approach. The killing of wolves would have to be constant in perpetuity—is that proper wildlife management, or even ethical? Ultimately, as repeated by biologists in countless reports commissioned by government wildlife agencies across the country, habitat protection is the only solution to most of our endangered or threatened wildlife species situations. Wolves often become a political scapegoat when certain prey species, which are also desired game species, have significant population decreases.

Wolves are remarkably adaptive, responding to opportunities in their habitat and reproducing to a population size largely governed by prey availability, which is why non-strategic culling is usually unsuccessful. Population dynamics of wolf and moose in Isle Royale National Park show decades of balance with no human impact. If wolf numbers are reduced and there is a large stock of ungulates for hunters, wolf packs could have large and even multiple litters in response to the larger available food source. In addition, if culling breaks apart pack structure, the once-larger pack could branch into several smaller packs, each producing pups and resulting in a population increase. More importantly, studies show that colonizing wolves take more elk calves than established packs do, as a result of weaker hunting skills. Lone wolves seek out more vulnerable prey, including livestock calves. According to the National Research Council (1997), long-term effectiveness of predator-control programs is questionable because wolf numbers rebound quickly.

The perceptions that the wolf is a threat to livestock, a hunting competitor for game and an unjustifiable risk to human safety have influenced the government for decades to control or eliminate wolves. The general public, meanwhile, went from passively condoning wolf extermination to quietly appreciating the wolf to crying out in its defence. Wolves became less vilified, and more Canadians are advocates for wolf conservation, seeking long-term solutions rather than continuous wolf culling to compensate for bad management of Canadian wilderness. We could see the wolf return to its former natural systems with contemporary wildlife restoration and management paradigms, if habitat protection is given priority over industrial development and reasonable conflict mitigation is implemented in agricultural areas.

HUNTING AND TRAPPING

Wolves have dual status as both game species and fur bearers throughout most Canadian jurisdictions, which means that they are managed but that not all wolves killed by people need be reported, depending on whether the circumstances are commercial or private. Under the Constitution, First Nations have the right to harvest wildlife for traditional use. In certain jurisdictions, such as in the territories, aboriginal harvest is open and unrestricted unless a particular species has a sensitive status. The wolf has sensitive status in Nunavut and harvest must be reported for statistical purposes, but there are no limitations for native harvest. Other species may be under a quota or limit whereby tags are required; for example, polar bear harvest is under a quota system and native hunters require tags. Export permits from the Convention on International Trade in Endangered Species of Wild Fauna and Flora (CITES) are required before transporting a grey wolf out of Canada.

To summarize, according to CITES Environment Canada, "Jurisdictional management strategies for grey wolf are reviewed annually and involve regulatory controls as well as management plans. Harvest seasons are established by management units and vary across jurisdictions from 'no closed season' to 'no open season' with an average open season of 9 to 10 months. The harvest may also be monitored by mandatory carcass submissions, reporting or questionnaires. In areas where there is some concern about grey wolf, seasons and harvest areas may be more restrictive and bag limits or quotas may be applied. For example, Ontario implemented a closed summer hunting and trapping season, and a maximum allowable harvest of two wolves/coyotes per hunter in 2005 and Quebec implements a shorter open season in wildlife management areas where trapping and hunting activities are permitted."

Hunting and trapping are still a part of many Canadians' lifestyles. Subsistence lifestyles are rare but do exist to some

degree, particularly in the North. Most Canadian hunters and trappers are connected to communities with modern and diverse amenities but profit from additional hunting or trapping. Native hunters and trappers are not required but encouraged to report their harvest so that management agencies can make loose estimates on population size. Private landowners are not limited to how many wolves they kill if on or near their property, but are required to report the kill; however, enforcement is minimal. Wolves are not long out of the category of vermin in Canada, and there may be lingering sentiments. For the most part, though, wolves have economic value and sustainable management is supported. The wolf population is considered able to sustain liberal regulations across the country.

The Modern Fur Trade in Canada

According to 2006 statistics, the Canadian fur industry generates an annual revenue of $800 million to add to Canada's GDP from its base of at least 60,000 trappers, about a third of which are aboriginal, as well as fur farmers, manufacturers and related enterprises involved in the Canadian fur trade. Of the $800 million, $300 million is in fur garment sales while only $25 million is in raw wild pelts. There is $78 million in farmed fur, particularly mink and fox. The remainder is estimated to be from related spin-off industries. When comparing industries in Canada, most of which are based upon raw resources, the fur industry yields a greater economic return on a parcel of land that is trapped versus the same piece of land that is consumed by the forestry industry. If properly managed, trapping is a long-term, sustainable industry that preserves habitat, compared with forestry practices that often decimate habitat in a one-time conversion of forest to tree farm.

However, the fur industry is in constant flux as international fashion tastes change, and the public perception of fur remains controversial. According to Statistics Canada, the fur industry grew from $51 million in wholesale shipments in 1970 to $170 million in 1978 (of which $81 million was exported) and to about $320 million in 1992 (of which $207 million was exported). According to Industry Canada, fur exports increased 44.3% between 1999 and 2004, from $250.1 million to $360.9 million.

Approximately 80% of Canadian fur goes to the United States, with Russia, Western Europe, China, Japan and Korea having the next highest demands. Fur sales are linked to major stock exchanges, such as Tokyo, Toronto and New York, and when economies are strong in these markets, fur demand increases. However, the industry is in decline, regardless of what the trapper associations' revenues might suggest. Animalrights.net collated data from 1980 and reported that 5.5 million animals were trapped that year in Canada. In 2003, Statistics Canada reported that less than a million (911,250) wild Canadian pelts were sold; in 2008, 741,769 pelts were sold. The total number of pelts taken, supply, sale price and demand gives an indication of the strength of the market and who is sustaining that market.

Wolf fur is still a common textile in fashion and function. In the Canadian North, a wolf fur–lined parka hood is the common standard. Today, the arctic wolf fur is the most highly prized pelt; unusual colour variances, such as the "blue" wolf, will call a premium price.

Table 3: The Canadian Fur Industry

- People in the fur trade:
  - 60,000 trappers (including aboriginal communities)
  - 2000 people in fur farming
  - 2500 people in manufacturing and processing
  - 2500 people in retailing
  - 1000 people in related services

- Production:
  - more than 2 million pelts produced annually in Canada; roughly half are farmed
  - wild furs: muskrat (35%), beaver (22%) and marten (17%); others include wolf, coyote, fox, squirrel and raccoon
  - farmed furs: mink, fox, chinchilla

- Major facilities:
  - fur garment manufacturing: Montreal (80%) and Toronto
  - fur dressing: Montreal and Winnipeg
  - auction: Toronto, North Bay and Vancouver

Figures used with the permission of the Fur Council of Canada.

Table 4: Canadian Wolf Pelts Sold in 2008

Province/Territory	Number of Pelts Sold	Total Value of Pelts Sold
British Columbia	115	$14,901
Alberta	276	$29,722
Saskatchewan	320	$45,034
Manitoba	443	$61,475
Ontario	439	$19,290
Quebec	617	$70,091
Labrador	47	$6613
Yukon	172	$28,896
Northwest Territories	96	$13,247
Nunavut	224	$62,213
Total	2749	$351,482

Figures from Statistics Canada 2010.

Prices for wolf pelts have fluctuated over the years and generally are determined by auction based on quality. For example, in Alberta, 1930–46 prices averaged $12 per wolf pelt, with an annual average harvest of 360 pelts. Prices dropped significantly during 1947–58, especially taking inflation into consideration, when the average pelt price was $5, and the harvest fell, with only 115 pelts marketed annually. The number sold on the market does not accurately reflect what was trapped; trappers discard pelts with mange, and some pelts would be kept for personal use or sold or traded privately. Actual harvest is recorded on fur affidavits (reports of fur animals taken). Fur prices shot up again in the late 1970s to early '80s, probably tied to some fashion trend: pelt prices averaged $70–$90 and went as high as $124 in 1978–79. However, the harvest did not seem to rise accordingly: 1972–84 saw an annual average of 556 pelts on the market. According to the 1991 Alberta Management Plan, an annual average of 388 wolves were reportedly captured over the last 10-year survey, but "trappers complain of difficulty of capture and that costs of capture, thawing, skinning and pelt preparation exceed market value."

In the 2008–09 season, 276 wolf pelts were reported as harvested in Alberta, at a mean price per pelt of $107.69 ($29,722.44 altogether). There were 18,965 coyote pelts reported at $39.29 per pelt, totalling $745,134.85. There was a peak harvest of 803 wolves in 2006. According to Roubichaud, between 1985 and 2006, 10,140 wolves were trapped on 1046 registered traplines in Alberta.

The trapping industry in Saskatchewan generates approximately $2.46 million in revenue annually (the mean of 1996–2005) through raw fur sales, with about 3200 registered trappers.

Fur returns in Ontario reflect an approximate 650 wolves killed by trappers per year, with an unknown additional number trapped or snared but with poor pelt quality.

Harvest statistics between 1992 and 2009 in the Northwest Territories (which included Nunavut until 1999) show an average annual harvest (declared pelts for trade) of about 105.5 wolves per year (range of 54–175); the average price per pelt was $199 (range of $144–$297). In 2009, pelts fetched on average of $138.

Two factors have influenced the number of pelts taken per year. Trapping has seen a decrease owing to the aging population of trappers and the low recruitment of young people into this way of life. For example, of Manitoba's 7500 registered trappers in 2006, 60% were aging aboriginals, Métis or non-status. The Fur Institute of Canada (FIC) implemented programs in communities in northern Manitoba to encourage teaching hunting, fishing and trapping skills to young people. Quebec has implemented similar public information campaigns promoting fishing and hunting, with perceived increases of interest among young people. According to Alberta Sustainable Resource Development, the number of Métis and First Nations trappers in Alberta has declined steadily, with a 75% decrease between 1994–95 and 2006–07.

Precise statistics on the percentage of aboriginal (status, non-status, Métis, etc.) hunters and trappers throughout Canada are lacking because fur sales are not classed or recorded by race of the producer, and it is arbitrary whether or not trappers identify themselves as native. Also, not all hunting and trapping is licensed or registered throughout Canada, with harvest unrecorded if for personal use. The Government of Canada estimates that up to half of trappers in Canada are aboriginal and derive a significant portion of their income from trapping.

The second factor that negatively influenced the harvest of fur-bearing animals was the 1991 European Union ban of all wild fur imports from any country using leghold traps. There was a five-year time limit imposed, but Canada obtained an extension by threatening action under the General Agreement on Tariffs and Trade (GATT). In 1997, the United States filed for action under the World Trade Organization, which ruled that no country should interfere in the trade practices of another on moral or ethical issues alone. That same year, Canada, Russia and the EU signed the Agreement on International Humane Trapping Standards (AIHTS), and a similar agreement was signed by the EU and the United States. Canada and the United States negotiated a trapping agreement in 1998 seeking permanent exemption from the fur ban. As a result of all these agreements, leghold traps now have to be of a particular design to not cause excessive damage or pain to the trapped animal; nonetheless, traps often leave animals to starve or freeze to death before being found. Trappers are allowed to let several days go by before they check their traps (for example, up to five days can pass before a trapper is required to check for a captured animal in the Yukon). The EU ban caused a shift from wild trapping to fur farming. Today fur farming in Canada is mainly for mink (with two-thirds of mink harvest being farmed fur and one-third wild harvest).

The public perception of furs remains in flux. Farming rather than trapping wild animals appeased certain groups of people, with the ideology that farming for fur is no different than farming for meat and leather. However, animal rights groups have used the Internet to expose the inhumane conditions farmed animals are reared in and the way they are killed (foxes, for example, are killed by anal electrocution, the brutal images and film footage of which are not for the squeamish). There is also the questionable waste of fur production when the rest of the animal—the carcass and meat—goes to waste; carcasses of wild-caught animals are returned to the bush for scavengers, and farmed animals are disposed of or rendered. Wolves are not farmed, only trapped in the wild.

Hunting and Trapping Regulations

Canada has fairly lax hunting regulations on wolves. In much of Canada, residents do not require a licence to shoot wolves. Trapping is fairly well regulated; trappers are required to register their traplines and report pelt sales. This system contrasts the system in Alaska, where trappers can harvest anywhere they choose as long as they follow area-specific regulations and seasons. Hunting is prohibited in Canadian national parks but most provincial parks allow it. In many jurisdictions, bait may only be used when hunting for wolves or coyotes.

British Columbia

British Columbia designated the wolf as a big game animal in 1966, affording it seasonal protection through provincial licensed hunting regulations, and as a furbearer in 1976, allowing for the regulation of wolf trapping. The BC Trappers Association receives annual grants from the Guide Outfitters Association of BC and the BC Wildlife Federation to establish wolf-trapping incentives. Wolf hunting and trapping seasons are defined by and vary between regions. Residents don't require a licence to hunt wolves, and non-residents can get a hunting licence for $50. As of 2010, a trapping licence is $40 and a royalty of $3.12 must be paid for each pelt. Native hunters and trappers are exempt from all licence and royalty obligations and are not obliged to report their harvest. For non-native hunters and trappers, the bag limit is typically three (though this number may vary between regions from one to three to unlimited).

Wolves can be shot with centrefire (not rimfire) rifles, shotguns and bows, and trapped with killing and foot snares, leghold traps and live box traps. Electronic or recorded calls for trapping wolves and coyotes are permitted. Baiting is permitted at specified times of year. Snares have to be at proper heights and loop sizes to not inhumanely catch target and non-target species; they cannot be used outside of bear hibernation periods. Private landowners can kill (shoot, trap, snare or poison) problem wolves—or any wolf on or near their property that is perceived to be a threat—but must report the incident.

Alberta

Wolves were classified as a fur-bearing carnivore in 1964 and as a game species in 1991 in Alberta. In 1987 all wolf hunting licence requirements for residents were dropped and wolf hunting on private property can occur year-round. Since 1975, non-residents are required to get a licence, for a minimal fee, to hunt wolves on public lands, but only during a specified season—typically through the winter, September to May, although seasons and bag limits vary throughout the province. As of 2010, setting out bait to solicit wolves to hunt them is lawful, except during spring black bear season.

A licence is required to trap wolves; a regulated trapping season (September 1 to April 31) was established in 1967. Furbearer harvest is managed through a registered trapline system established in 1939 to eliminate competition between trappers. Alberta has approximately 1700 registered traplines across eight fur management zones; the size of these management areas ranges from 3 km^2 to 4415 km^2. Wolves can be trapped with leghold traps or Belisle foot snares.

Saskatchewan

Wolves are considered a furbearer in Saskatchewan. A hunter must have a fur licence and be within an area with an open season to harvest them. The fur licence costs $30 in the South Saskatchewan Open Trapping Area and $10 in the Northern Fur Conservation Block. There is no hunting season in Saskatchewan per se: wolves can be shot as a means of harvest but only under the authority of the fur regulations. Conventional leghold traps were banned in April 2001; only traps with offset or padded jaws may now be used. Livestock producers may shoot, snare or trap a problem wolf on their land at any time of the year but must report the kill to Saskatchewan Environment, which retrieves the carcass: wolves are protected wildlife and the property of the government agency.

Manitoba

In Manitoba, wolves and coyotes can be hunted with a big game licence. Tags are species specific; for example, the licence with a moose tag allows that hunter to only shoot a moose. However, a hunter may kill a single wolf with any big game species tag (deer, moose, elk, caribou or bear). There is a bizarre rule: if a hunter has, for example, an elk tag and sees a wolf, the hunter can kill the wolf and continue stalking elk and subsequently also take the elk; however, if the elk walks into the scope first and is shot, the wolf hunt is over. This apparently prevents hunters who have already used their game tag on an ungulate going out with other hunters with unused tags and stalking ungulates but claiming that they are just wolf hunting. The hunting season varies per game species and method of hunting (rifle, archery, bait hunting, etc.) throughout the winter, but continues year-round for coyotes and wolves. The season for a wolf-specific tag is from August 30 to March 31. Non-resident hunters must have an unused game tag to hunt wolf or coyote, and foreign hunters must be accompanied by a guide. Trapping is for Manitoba residents only, on registered traplines with a $10 licence or in an open area with a $5 licence. There is no charge for a Treaty open area licence.

Ontario

In Ontario, wolves and coyotes (or hybrids) are classified as furbearing mammals and can be harvested by individual hunters and trappers under a licence to hunt small game or a trapping licence. Hunters in wolf range must purchase a wolf game seal (which is like a tag) in addition to the licence, with a limit of two game seals per year. There is no limit on trapping during open season. The hunting and trapping season within wolf range is September 15 to March 31, except in 40 townships around Algonquin Provincial Park where hunting and trapping has been closed since 2001. The season is open year-round outside of traditional wolf range (to the south).

Ontario is the only province where regulations intended to protect wolves apply to coyotes as well. Coyotes are difficult to distinguish from wolves, especially eastern wolves, where their ranges overlap. It is mandatory for all hunters, trappers and landowners to report all wolf or coyote kills. Pelts taken for trade must be reported by taxidermists and fur buyers, but because of hybridization and the similarities between eastern wolves and coyotes, the actual number of harvested eastern wolves versus coyotes is unknown.

For the purpose of field-training hunting dogs, wolves can be chased even in the closed season (Licence to Chase Raccoon at Night and Fox, Coyote and Wolf During the Day) except around Algonquin. No firearms are permitted during the chase.

Wolves are protected from hunting in all provincial parks, but trapping is permitted in nearly half of the provincial parks. Wolves are fully protected in Algonquin Provincial Park, Lake Superior Provincial Park, Pukaskwa National Park and all provincial reserves such as the Nipissing Crown Game Preserve and the Chapleau Crown Game Preserve. However, wolves are frequently killed by humans when they exit the arbitrary boundaries of these protected areas.

Quebec

Wolves have furbearer status in Quebec, and a small game licence is required to hunt them and a general trapping licence to trap them. Hunting and trapping seasons change with zones. Since 1984, wolf hunting and trapping has been managed with controlled hunting and trapping seasons, but reporting of wolf harvest is not required.

Labrador

Wolves have game and furbearer status in Labrador. They may be harvested from October 15 to April 30 in the northern zone of Labrador, and from November 1 to April 30 in the southern zone. Hunters may purchase a licence to shoot a wolf for $25, which permits harvest of a single wolf. As furbearers, wolves may be harvested on a general trapper licence ($10), to which there is no limit on harvest.

Nunavut

Wolves are a big game animal in Nunavut, and non-Inuit hunters are required to obtain a hunting licence to harvest them. The tag fee is $10 per tag for residents, $20 per tag for Canadian non-residents and $50 per tag for foreign non-residents. Non-residents (including foreigners) have a single animal bag limit and a trophy fee of $100. The territory is divided into three hunting zones (N1, N2 and N3). The hunting season is August 15 to May 31 and only in hunting zones N2 and N3. Nunavut residents are also permitted to hunt in zone N3 during that season and in zones N1 and N2 between September 1 and May 15. Inuit hunters require no licence and have no bag limit or any other restrictions (prey age, prey sex, season or hunting zone), whereas non-Inuit hunters are not permitted to hunt baby or juvenile animals or pregnant females and have to comply with zones and season restrictions.

Northwest Territories

In the Northwest Territories, wolves are classified as both a big game species and a furbearer, and therefore can be hunted or trapped. There is no bag limit for residents. Wolf hunting and trapping is restricted to winter in an effort to protect wolves when they are raising pups and when their fur is not in prime condition. The annual harvest averages around 915 pelts while harvests have occasionally been as high as 1500–2000 animals (1998), causing concern with environmentalists and wildlife officials. According to wildlife experts, the high kill rates were influenced by high international demand for wolf fur, and by hunters' use of snowmobiles to drive wolves into the open where they are sometimes run to exhaustion. This hunting style has caused criticism and controversy, with demands for humane regulation of the hunt. The Northwest Territories allows hunting on snowmobiles, and there are no limits on how many wolves can be killed.

Yukon

Wolves are classified as big game in the Yukon. Up until the 1990s there was no closed season, bag limit or requirement for hunting tags; today residents must have a game licence ($10 resident, $75 Canadian non-resident, $150 foreign). Each licence year, residents may harvest seven wolves and non-residents may harvest two wolves. The hunting season runs year-round, from April 1 to March 31. Trapping season for wolves is November 1 to March 10 (neck snare only from March 11 to March 31), with licences costing $10 (free for seniors). Trapping for fur is reportedly low owing to low pelt value. The pelt of a harvested wolf must be submitted to a Conservation Officer within 15 days of the kill or before the pelt is sold or transferred, and incurs a $10 handling (sealing) fee. Native and Inuit hunters and trappers do not require licences, nor do they have bag limits. The 1992 Yukon Wolf Conservation and Management Plan states that the annual wolf harvest is 3–6% of the estimated population.

OTHER CONTROL METHODS

Aerial sport hunting has been met with public outrage, resulting in bans that are then again rescinded when pressure from hunters increases. Recreation aerial hunting is ongoing in Alaska, but it is not permitted for sport in Canada. However, wildlife managers in BC, Alberta, the Northwest Territories and periodically other jurisdictions cull wolves by aerial shooting from either planes or helicopters. Shooting is often in combination with poisoning, with poison being airdropped at times (in the '50s and '60s local governmental wildlife agencies airdropped poison-laced bait to kill wolves). BC and Alberta have sterilized breeding pairs of specific packs.

Hunting from snowmobiles is common practice in the territories and in certain other jurisdictions, such as the Northwest Territories. In Saskatchewan, a landowner may obtain a permit to pursue a problem wolf by snowmobile. However, the firearm may not be carried loaded or discharged from the vehicle. The animal may not be injured or killed by the use of the snowmobile alone.

There are ethical questions surrounding wolf control. For instance, is it humane to allow a highly social animal such as a wolf to watch its mate or offspring be killed or lie dying in a snare, or writhing from poisoning? John and Mary Theberge radio-collared wolves in Algonquin Provincial Park for decades, and described the pity one could not help but feel for a particular immature male wolf they had collared. Over a period of a few months, that wolf suffered the anguish of observing its entire pack wiped out by being shot by humans. The chances of its survival were slim, and they knew it would suffer a potentially long, lonely existence until its own death. If we acknowledge mental and emotional trauma in dogs that have been abused or frightened, or the lethargy we see in a dog that loses its master, or in a dog that is kept in a cage void of social interaction (we won't refer to sadness or depression for risk of anthropomorphizing), it is not so implausible to consider the emotional trauma our management practices have on individual surviving wolves.

Aerial Shooting

Wolves are normally elusive, but aerial hunting puts wolves at a complete disadvantage: they have to outrun an airplane and avoid being shot with a high-powered rifle with a scope. It is now illegal in Canada to shoot to kill wolves from planes, except by government wildlife officials or with a permit issued specifically to target problem wolves, as is the case in Saskatchewan. However, Helen Thayer reports that illegal activities continue in remote areas. Some people shoot directly from planes, or chase the wolves and shoot in their vicinity to keep them running into open areas until the animals collapse from exhaustion, at which point the hunters land the plane and easily shoot the wolves from the ground.

It seems that wolves have learned to fear the sky, from where there was no natural threat throughout their evolution. Thayer observed wolf pups in areas where aerial shooting or stalking had occurred in the Yukon and documented them looking skyward when she could see no sign of ravens or other birds. She deducted that they had learned from unnatural, life-threatening events in the past to keep diligent surveillance of the skies. In her book *Three Among the Wolves*, she observed an adult wolf teaching pups to look skyward. It would cock its head upward repeatedly until the pups mimicked him. When a plane was subsequently heard in the area, the wolf would look skyward and the pups would do the same. Thayer concluded that the pups were learning what to watch for and could be seen implementing this behaviour whenever a plane was heard. The ability to teach offspring survival tactics indicates the wolf's intelligence.

Thayer confirmed that the planes she saw in her study site held guides with hunters. When the planes passed over the territory of the wolves she was studying, the pack heard the sound of the plane engine and retreated into hiding. They remained reclusive long after the plane had left the area, and it took five days for them to resume their regular hunting routines.

In other areas where only government biologists and wildlife wardens are permitted to aerial-shoot wolves, the officials sometimes shoot from helicopters. This is a costly management regime—hiring aircraft and paying for fuel is not financially feasible for agencies that claim not to have the funds to conduct population surveys. In the past, funding has come from private associations with vested interests. For example, biologists were equipped with shotguns and flown over BC's Muskwa-Kechika area in the 1980s with financial backing from the US trophy hunting association Foundation for North American Wild Sheep. Hundreds of wolves were killed per year in this fashion alone. In 1983, 283 wolves were killed by the aerial hunting campaign in one winter within a 14,000 km² "wolf removal area" in northeastern BC. The aerial shooting stopped in 1986, resumed briefly in 1987 and then ceased after public protest and a successful court case challenge. The Disney film *Never Cry Wolf* was shot in the Muskwa-Kechika area in 1983. Tony Brummet, the BC Environment Minister at the time, portrayed wolves as "vicious, wasteful and unrelenting killers," demonstrating that there was wolf hatred even within the conservation department at the time.

Poisoning

Shooting wolves from planes and helicopters can prove to be difficult, particularly in areas that are heavily forested or where wolves cannot be easily spotted. In such areas, wildlife officials use poison to control wolf populations. The use of compound 1080 and strychnine have been banned from many provinces, but are still in use in western Canada as controlled toxins.

Compound 1080 is a synthetic organofluorine compound—sodium monofluoroacetate—that is still in use today to kill wolves in Alberta and Saskatchewan. Although it is banned in the United States and Mexico, compound 1080 can be used by provincial authorities, or their designated representatives, to control wolves and coyotes. It is banned in most countries, though this poison remains the control method of choice in countries such as New Zealand, which has a campaign to eradicate all exotic mammal species, mainly rodents, except of course for deliberately introduced ungulates for game and livestock. Compound 1080 is a controlled substance in Canada and can only be used on problem wolves by government officials who are licensed to use specific quantities. According to Health Canada, BC no longer uses compound 1080, but up until recently BC had the authority to use ¼ oz. annually on problem wildlife, which is enough to kill 800 canines through primary poisoning and enough to kill many more animals through secondary poisoning. It is estimated that 15% of bait is taken by non-target animals, non-problem wolves and other species, and those carcasses then secondarily poison scavengers such as birds or prey, small carnivores such as weasels and other large predators such as bears, cougars, coyotes and foxes. Compound 1080 is a persistent compound and cannot (or should not) be used near water sources or human settlement. It is a male reproductive toxin linked with endocrine dysfunction.

Compound 1080 induces an extremely painful death. It is a slow killer, taking up to 48 hours to kill an ungulate, 21 hours for carnivores. During those hours the animal suffers an agonizing death that commences with rapid, laboured breathing, choking, salivating and incontinence and culminates in seizures and convulsions, with eyes rolling back and teeth clenching. Those who have witnessed these deaths say the animal is apparently in extreme anxiety and terror, vocalizing its pain.

Strychnine poisoning attacks the central nervous system, causing similar effects as 1080 poisoning: anxiety, muscle stiffness, convulsions, panting and sometimes nausea and vomiting. The symptoms increase in severity, coinciding with extreme pain. Strychnine is a potent poison to all animals—including humans. The victim does not lose consciousness initially but first succumbs to seizures. These become more severe and longer lasting as the poison becomes absorbed into the system. Finally the victim will lose consciousness when tonic rigidity of the respiratory muscles causes apnea and then cerebral anoxia. If respiration restarts, the victim may revive only to endure a repeat process of seizure and suffocation.

Using strychnine to poison wildlife is infrequent now in certain US states such as Michigan, owing to its classification as a restricted pesticide with limited use by certified applicators only. This restriction came in part from public pressure after too many accidental pet poisonings. It is still used in western Canada by wildlife officials to poison problem wildlife.

Jim Pissot, executive director of Defenders of Wildlife Canada, says Albertans do not want to see wolves pay the price for provincial mismanagement of their wildlife. He says strychnine poisoning is a "painful and horrible way to die."

Sterilization

The Yukon, BC and Alberta have used sterilization as part of their wolf control programs in recent years. A University of Alberta sterilization project has been endorsed by the Alberta government and supported by the Alberta Fish and Game Association, but has been criticized by Parks Canada and has received mixed reviews from individual biologists, conservationists, hunters, trappers and members of the general public.

In theory, the concept of sterilizing breeding pairs is a humane alternative to lethal control. All males in select packs could be sterilized to reduce the biotic potential of wolf populations. It is unknown how a pack responds when it doesn't produce offspring. The pack order could disrupt and disperse to find alternative mates. A prominent wolf expert, David Mech, did a 1996 study in Minnesota and found that five wild male wolves from four packs continued to hold mates and territories despite not producing offspring. However, owing to the long-term nature of population dynamics, it is impossible to say whether such a scheme would hold. The sterilization option, which has obvious labour costs, aims to sterilize the breeding pair (if positively identifiable, and again assuming this hierarchy would not shift after unsuccessful reproduction) and kill the other members of the pack, including the pups. Paul Paquet, a prominent and expert wolf researcher, zoologist and author, calls the experiment "destructive and morally reprehensible." Jim Pissot, executive director of Defenders of Wildlife Canada, told the *Calgary Herald* that, "There's certainly an ethical and moral dimension of murdering all pups and sub-adults in a pack, sterilizing the alpha pair and sitting back to see what happens." He furthers that the program is a "bone-headed wolf cull poorly disguised as research."

Some voices urge us to remember that the reason for culling wolves is not that the species is overpopulating but that habitat loss is threatening the survival of certain prey species.

So, again, is it ethical to target the wolves for human misman-agement of habitat? Parks Canada defends its opposition to wolf control, reminding us that wolf control in the 1960s, which aimed to increase prey densities, caused unnaturally high prey densities and problems that persist to this day.

Nevertheless, a five-year project was proposed in 2008, but cancelled then reproposed in 2010, on a pack of wolves near Rocky Mountain House, Alberta (approximately 230 km north-west of Calgary and 215 km southwest of Edmonton). These wolves are already subjected to hunting and trapping, which aims to increase elk populations for hunters. The sterilization of four more wolf packs near Rocky Mountain House was ongo-ing in 2010, as well as additional packs in central Alberta that prey on sensitive caribou populations. The project is being repeated in the foothills, where the Little Smokey woodland caribou herd is suffering significant declines from rapid habitat loss that exposes them to increased wolf depredation. Similar sterilization plans have been implemented in the Muskwa-Kechika area of BC's northern Rockies solely for the purpose of increasing hunting opportunities for moose and elk.

In the years since the first project commenced, biolo-gists, wolf researchers and environmental and conservation organizations have commented on the dubious efficacy of wolf sterilization. They question whether breeding pairs are correctly identified, and the likelihood that the breeding pair changes from year to year, making sterilization ineffec-tive. The pack disruption from this program while continued wolf harvest has taken place has actually seen wolf popula-tion increases. To be at all effective, sterilization requires stable pack structure; in none of the current sterilization schemes is this stability permitted, owing to either continued hunting and trapping or deliberate killing of pups and other pack members.

In most sterilization schemes, the rest of the pack is destroyed, leaving a pack of only two. There are inherent prob-lems here: either the pack invites in lone wolves, increasing the pack size back to near average sizes and also introducing the possibility that these lone wolves will become producers, or the two surviving wolves may be killed by other wolves. It is very unlikely that a pack will remain with only two members, since two is not a natural pack size for this social species, particularly when it comes to hunting strategy. A pack of only two wolves would have more difficulty taking down large game such as elk and may resort to easier, more vulnerable prey, which could be endangered caribou or livestock.

Vasectomies and uterine horn ligations were performed on wild wolves in the Yukon in the '90s to research the effects of sterilization. Two females died, one from the capture procedure and the other from post-surgery infection; another female wolf produced a litter.

There is one final question to consider: is the removal of reproductive organs of a wild wolf ethical or morally defensible?

A crucial point is that good science rests on good ethics. What scientists do matters; it counts ethically.

—B. Jickling and P.C. Paquet

Mitigating the Impact of Wolves

Wolves have a right to be here, but like rats, they sometimes impinge on what man wants to do.

—Don Robinson, BC Wildlife Federation

Livestock Depredation

I remember worrying about "my" coyotes being shot by certain neighbouring farmers who didn't like coyotes being around. There are varying levels of appreciation and tolerance among rural people with predators such as coyotes and wolves. Many Canadian farmers, horse ranchers and small acreage owners with beautiful landscaping appreciate the coyotes for keeping down the population of "gophers" (actually Richardson's ground squirrels). I understood that nobody wanted their livestock or pets preyed upon—I had lost pets to coyotes, as well as to weasels, hawks and unconfirmed night-time stalkers. Many people who grew up in rural Canada can relate. I would do my best to prevent losing a pet to a wild predator and be upset if it happened, but understood the risk of living in the countryside. I realized that animals are animals, all part of the circle of life. I am one of those Canadians who would need to see an exceptional situation to justify killing coyotes, wolves or other wild predators.

Looking at the distribution of wolves on the Canadian range map (see p. 12), the mainland has a continuous blanket of wolf presence except for one nasty, conspicuous hole on the southern prairies, a lasting scar from earlier days of wolf extermination policies on both sides of the border. With increased appreciation of wolves and improved mitigation policies, wolves may return to their former range as they edge into southwestern Alberta with natural migration from the Rocky Mountains. Wolf packs that enter the zone south of the Bow River to the Montana border often do not survive owing to liberal hunting and trapping regulations and land-owners' right to shoot on sight wolves on or near their property. There is a constant battle between natural and artificially introduced systems. Just as farmers and ranchers are waged in a constant battle against weeds and insects, they also fight the encroaching mammals, whether they are ground squirrels or wolves. The cycle of wolf depredation, wolf cull, wolf recovery back to wolf depredation continues to turn its squeaky, ineffective wheel. More and more animals are killed with every rotation unless other mitigation techniques are implemented for sustainable, long-term cohabitation of wildlife adjacent to or in agricultural areas.

The Canadian identity in the West prides itself on the honest work of the rancher. Though cattle have an impact on natural grasslands, they have at the same time prevented unprotected grasslands from being converted to grain crops. Much overdue scrutiny of overpopulated feedlots and a consumer demand for grass-fed beef requires acreage. Canada now exports beef to China and other countries. Producing beef to feed the world requires millions more cattle on the open prairies. Sustainability and wildlife conservation are big issues.

Depredation of livestock by wolves happens, often with serious financial losses to ranchers. In Alberta, from 1972 to 1990, there were 2800 claims of harassment, injury or killing of livestock or pets made to wildlife management authorities:

- cattle: 73%
- horses: 6%
- sheep: 5%
- dogs: 7%
- bison: 2%
- poultry: 2%
- goats: 1%
- other: 4%

Most ranchers who suffer from livestock losses to wolves are in agricultural zones adjacent to forested areas in the foothills and river drainages, the forest–agricultural fringe. This fringe is extensive in Alberta, where the western border of Canada's prairies reaches the foothills of the Rocky Mountains. Alberta's foothills have high industrial, commercial and residential development. Ungulates pushed out of their foothill habitat onto agricultural lands will lead wolves to livestock. Grazing reserves and leased pastures in forested public lands, where wolves can be abundant, have high-incident ratios of livestock depredation. Increased animal husbandry, shepherding and common sense are necessary to protect cattle and

mitigate losses, with only occasional habituated or problem wolves likely needing to be shot—not a total extermination of the species. A rancher has to take the responsibility of checking the herd daily: to remove carcasses of dead cattle (dead cattle may be from diseases or accidents as well as from predation), to be present at dawn and dusk, when wolves are most likely to be stalking prey opportunities, and simply to be a frequent presence deterring human-shy predators such as wolves. Diligent night-riding or dusk/dawn human presence is especially warranted during the calving season. Afterbirth from newborn calves must be promptly removed and properly disposed of so it does not attract wolves or other predators. All this increased labour is costly. Is the public willing to pay more for beef that is raised with these efforts? How can the consumer know of these wilderness-friendly ranchers and directly support them?

Ranchers discard of livestock carcasses in pits called boneyards or in rendering piles. These attract predators to scavenge, which could result in habituated predators with a preference for this food source over their natural prey. It is not unreasonable that these carnivores would develop a taste for beef. Boneyards are typically as close as 400 m to livestock facilities and residences, inviting predators to come closer to livestock and increasing chances of predation. According to recent study (Morehouse 2010), 400 m is not much of a distance or deterrent to a large carnivore, given the potential benefits of finding prey.

Wolves can be successful at taking down adult cattle, but predation on calves is more common. Grazing lands are so large that bringing herds into paddocks at night is unfeasible. Many ranchers allow their cows to calve in the open fields, which is a huge risk. Subsequently, it had been common practise to leave yearling calves to free range (free-range beef is more desirable than feedlots for ethical and environmental reasons), but the predations rates are again higher on these young herds. Cow–calf pairs have lower predation rates; wolves don't have much success in separating calves from cows and tend not to even make the attempt. Cow–calf pairs group together in defence of approaching predators, much as wild ungulates do. Cows have been known to stand up to predators in defence of their calves.

There are also more aggressive breeds of cattle. Some livestock ranchers include longhorn steers in their herds, which have been known to discourage predators by aggressively charging at them! These steers can be effective shepherds, protecting calves and yearlings in the field. Corrientes and Brahman breeds show similar behaviour. Brahman cows crossed with Angus and Herefords (producing Brangus and Brafords) demonstrate aggression toward predators, have particularly strong mothering skills and maternal instincts to protect their young and are good beef producers with high reproductive success. Ranchers in southwestern Alberta have observed differences between what are coined "naïve" and "mountain-savvy" cows. Mountain-savvy cows, or cows familiar with mountainous terrain, appear to be less vulnerable to predation than cows raised on prairie pasture and moved seasonally to foothill areas for grazing. The naïve cows are unfamiliar with the foothill landscape and seem to lack the maternal instincts to defend calves from predators. It is an interesting possibility that mountain cows evolved some wildlife skills after a couple centuries of coexistence in wolf territory, whereas prairie cows lived predator free for the majority of that time. Indeed, if cows roam feral or semi-wild, will they not develop survival strategies just like any other ungulate? And is it not equally logical to assume that wolves should not be expected to see these feral cows as any less wild and fair game than the deer and elk in that habitat?

Multi-stakeholder groups, such as the Oldman Basin Carnivore Advisory Group and later the Southwestern Alberta Carnivore Advisory Group, have advised the Alberta government over the past several years on managing large carnivores in the prairies. These advisory groups have teamed up with conservationists, biologists, government policy makers and frustrated ranchers who want a long-term, sustainable and ecologically inclined solution to mitigate livestock losses from wolves. One rancher in this group was quoted as saying, "We keep doing what doesn't work...only harder." The groups analyze factors that may contribute to depredation, such as landscape features, wolf pack stability, availability of natural prey and livestock stewardship and predation mitigation methods, as well as the basic ecology, behaviour and movement of wolves in the area.

Many ranchers actually value wolves for their role in keeping down elk and deer populations that compete with cattle for grazing, and these ranchers will only shoot problematic wolves if attempts at non-lethal dissuasions do not work. One of the concerns of Alberta ranchers again regards habitat protection in the forest reserves and river drainages. Too much motorized recreation in these areas is displacing wildlife. Prey species are being pushed closer to ranches, and the predators follow. In addition, the overexploitation of oil and gas in Alberta is an ever-increasing counter to habitat protection.

The ranchers in the Willow Creek drainage area of southern Alberta coexisted with a resident pack of wolves that has gone after calves. Rather than immediately responding with a call to destroy the offending wolves, as had occurred in the past (such as the strychnine poisoning in 1990), the division, upon recommendation from the Oldman advisory group, contracted a biologist to capture and collar the wolves. The result was the proven identification of the offending pack and confirmation of its numbers (six adults and eight pups of the year). More importantly, the study delineated the pack's travel routes, den, rendezvous sites and pack territory, as well as identified the role of grizzly bears in the depredation scenario. Ranchers in the area were able to use telemetry equipment to determine where the wolves were and make decisions on their livestock management strategies by changing grazing and salt lick locations, spending more time shepherding on the range and harassing wolves they spotted near the cattle.

Despite these efforts, 28 losses (out of approximately 4000 head in the area) showed the depredation trend was continuing. The advisory group recommended commencing lethal control but with a systematic approach, rather than destroying the entire pack. Based on behavioural and social structures in the pack and the concept of teaching deterrence, the hope was that by selectively culling the pack, there was a long-term chance of the pack's survival. The alternative would be to eliminate this pack entirely, leaving the territory open for a new pack to repeat the same habits that had occurred in the area for years. It was not an easy, clean solution, but over two years, selected members of the pack were euthanized and the remaining members equipped with satellite collars. The captures took place when wolves returned to a depredation site; several members were captured together, euthanizing all but one who was released. This method hoped to teach consequences and create negative associations with cattle kill sites. New members joined the pack and new pups were born. This particular case study's final reports were of no depredation by that pack for 22 months.

Another case study involved a pack farther south at Bob Creek that was associated with the loss of 63 cattle over a five-year period. The breeding male was identified and removed from the pack and the remaining members collared and monitored, and no further depredation was observed in the following year. Since the dominant breeding male may not be the lead male in the hunt, biologists have to closely monitor the behaviour of the pack before implementing any mitigation that involves selective culling within a pack. Radio-collaring is now a permanent mitigation tool used by wildlife researchers and managers in cooperation with ranchers.

Now, after all this effort, industry may jeopardize the progress that has been made in Willow Creek. The Petro-Canada Sullivan Field development includes a 51 km trunk pipeline built through the Willow Creek pack's territory, traditional den site and pup-rearing areas. A report by wolf researchers in the area states that when the pipeline is built, the wolves will likely relocate and move closer to private land with livestock, and ultimately, wolf–cattle conflicts will occur. The Pekisko Group, an association of ranching families "dedicated to responsible stewardship of the ranchlands along the southeast slopes of the Rockies," argued that "the Project constituted unwarranted and damaging industrial intrusion into the Southern Foothills area" and opposed the development. The development was approved by the Alberta government in June 2010.

Livestock Compensation Programs

Throughout Canada, landowners have the right to shoot a wolf without hunting or trapping licences if the wolf is on or in proximity to the person's land or livestock. No loss of livestock is required justification; mere presence can validate threat. Because there are no penalties or repercussions for a landowner shooting a wolf, the wolf doesn't have to pose any threat, and if uncertain, the landowner could shoot just to eliminate the possibility. Like a form of insurance, compensation schemes recover some if not all of the financial loss a rancher incurs from wolf predation on livestock. Compensation programs also function to reduce hostility toward wolves and prevent vigilante-style extermination approaches that were the norm in the early pioneering days.

In southern Alberta, where there is an abrupt transition from forest to agricultural land, there is little in the way of a buffer to separate wolves from livestock. During the summer grazing season, roughly mid-May through mid-October, livestock graze on public lands where there are higher rates of wolf predation. The Alberta Conservation Association supports a livestock compensation program to reimburse ranchers for livestock losses caused by wolf predation. A Livestock Predator Compensation Program was initiated in Alberta in 1974. Today, a producer who loses livestock intended for meat (not pets and not animals reared for wool or other products) may file a claim with the local Fish and Wildlife division within three days of learning of a death or injury of that animal. Claims vary to compensate for the average market value of the loss or replacement of the same type and class of animal. The producer is compensated 100% of the market value for confirmed wolf kills and 50% for probable kills, but nothing for missing animals.

Kills are investigated to prove they were predatory, and to identify the cause of the predation and the degree of preventative measure that the livestock owner took. Claims paid out through Alberta's compensation program were $144,374.35 in 2009–10. In the past 10 years, total compensation, which includes depredation by bears, cougars and raptors as well as wolves, was $944,006.18; the total amount attributed solely to wolves was $703,829.29. Depredation of livestock is a problem throughout Alberta, but according to Morehouse (2010), a particular portion of southern Alberta, which is only 3% of the land mass, accounts for 37% of all paid claims.

Across the rest of the prairies, most livestock rearing takes place in areas from which wolves have been extirpated. Saskatchewan implemented a compensation scheme in 2010 in areas near the forest fringe that experienced high livestock depredation. This step is perhaps evidence that wolves are re-entering former wolf ranges from the north. Manitoba only compensates ranchers for predation by bears.

Ontario implemented the Wolf Damage to Livestock Compensation Act in the 1970s. This act does not give any trigger-happy individual permission to go out and shoot a wolf for a prize, but it does permit landowners to shoot wolves trespassing on their property and compensates ranchers with cash payments for damage or loss to livestock caused by wolves or coyotes. In email communication, the Ontario Ministry of Natural Resources says that "Under the Ontario Fish and Wildlife Conservation Act, landowners can take action against a canid that has damaged or is about to damage their property and to use an agent to do so on their behalf. Municipalities that are interested in assisting livestock producers with the removal of specific problem animals may also be authorized by the Ontario Ministry of Natural Resources to hire an agent on behalf of the landowner—authorization is provided only where there has been a documented predation incident and the control actions, the general area of control and the time period during which the control can occur must be approved by the ministry. Currently, Ontario pays compensation for livestock predation under the Livestock, Poultry and Honeybee Compensation Act administered by the Ontario Ministry of Agriculture, Food and Rural Affairs."

Ontario pays hundreds of thousands of dollars per year in compensation for livestock losses attributed to wolves and coyotes. The highest payouts are in coyote-only ranges or where both wolves and coyotes are present; most livestock losses are poultry. A high number of wild canids live in close proximity to farms, but only a fraction are implicated in livestock losses. Oftentimes one producer will be affected while neighbouring producers suffer no losses. The number of small pets, particularly cats, lost to predation has increased and, again, this is more likely coyote than wolf. Occasionally domestic dogs are killed by wolves in more remote areas.

Of course, livestock owners have to take personal responsibility to reduce the chances of depredation as much as possible. Increased human presence mitigates livestock depredation: livestock–predator interactions are reduced and the rancher can also quickly and efficiently remove attractants, such as sick, injured or dead livestock. Ranchers need to look and listen for signs of predator presence (tracks, scat, agitation of the herd, natural prey kills, howling), and if a loss should occur, contact officials immediately to investigate the range of conditions leading to the cause of the incident.

Fladry

One mitigation technique showing promising results is the use of fladry. Fladry is a type of flagging that originated in Europe. Lu Carbyn was the first Canadian biologist to write about the merits of fladry in 1977, after he visited eastern Poland for work with a Polish biologist, Piotr Suminski, a project that had been set up by Doug Pimlott. Carbyn observed the fladry technique first-hand and brought the technique to the attention of Canadian biologists and ranchers.

Fladry is a simple system: a single rope or wire at about mid-height of a wolf, with red flags staggered about 10–20 cm apart surrounding a paddock or pasture. The numerous, flapping red flags act as a psychological barrier that wolves are too skittish to cross over or under. (I do not know if the colour really matters, but red is consistently the colour I have seen used.) Some fladry uses an electric-charged wire—less for shocking the predator that likely won't approach the wire anyway and more to prevent livestock from chewing on the wire.

Fladry works especially well to protect sheep from wolves. In Montana, dozens of sheep had been depredated and two wolf packs destroyed before one rancher in the Red Lodge area decided to test the fladry technique. Wolf tracks in spring snow were seen leading to the paddock surrounded by the fladry: the wolves stopped near the flapping obstacle, turned back, reapproached from another angle, encountered the deterrent again and finally retreated. The rancher implemented an electric fence as an additional protection and moves the paddock around periodically. He has only lost one ewe to wolves since implementing the fladry in 2005—and that was only because the ewe was accidentally left outside of the pen.

Guard Dogs

Guard dogs have an effect in deterring wolves, particularly if the pasture is small enough that the dogs can establish and defend a territory. The training of a guard dog must begin at puppyhood, and specific breeds have the characteristics necessary for guarding. Herd dogs are not guard dogs (in other words, breeds such as border collies and sheepdogs are great herders but not great guard dogs, while Anatolian shepherds, Maremma sheepdogs and Great Pyrenees are natural livestock guard dogs that have long been used to ward off wolves in Europe). There has been much success with guard dogs deterring coyotes, foxes, bears and cougars, and protecting smaller livestock species such as sheep, llamas, goats and pigs; but the use of guard dogs for cattle in wolf country is not yet common, so fewer statistics on success rates are available. Some case studies show that guard dogs have been effective in deterring wolves, which are observed avoiding or bypassing the area occupied by guard dogs. However, other cases indicate that the wolves may be more frustrated by the dogs than deterred, and may attack the dogs. Livestock guard dogs are most effective to alert people of the presence of wolves. They can potentially deter wolves, but they do not fight against wolves. In fact, owners of guard dogs have to train them not to chase down or attack wolves. The dogs are also used in first response situations to notify owners of other predators, such as bears and cougars, as well as of prey carcasses of wolves or food caches of bear kills or other carrion, which can attract wolves.

Livestock guard dogs became more common in parts of Canada after the poison compound 1080 was banned from public use. Dogs were used to protect domestic sheep in forestry clear-cuts on Vancouver Island in the 1990s. The sheep were used in the clear-cuts to assist in brush control. Research (Rigg 2001) indicated the dogs reduced the predation rates by wolves as well as by bears and cougars.

Night Rides

The Oldman Basin Carnivore Advisory Group proved that night rides were a successful form of livestock shepherding, though expensive and involving many man-hours. Ranchers monitored collared wolves entering areas where cattle were out to pasture and sent out night riders to deter the wolves from the area. Firework gangers, screamers and gunshots were fired toward (but not at) the wolves to deter them. During the period of study, signals from collared wolves were detected, night riders deployed and wolves deterred on nine evenings. No cattle were lost. During the study period, adjacent lands with no use of this shepherding method suffered livestock losses from wolves, proving the efficacy of night riding.

Radio-collared Wolves

Wildlife managers, conservation organizations and ranchers have collaborated for years to mitigate livestock losses and still allow wolves to inhabit ranching lands. Radio-collaring wolves in problem packs has been ongoing in southern Alberta for years. Not only does the radio-collar allow people to follow the movements of the wolves and give a method for monitoring their movements and proximity to herds, but it can also be used in conjunction with other mitigation technologies. A radio-activated guard system (called a RAG box) sets off flashing strobe lights and loud alarm sounds when the wolf collar comes into proximity of the box. The RAG box can be installed in the field to a fence or other structure and has the additional bonus of having a small computer that collects information from the collar—such as the specific frequency of a collar, which then identifies the specific wolf or wolf pack, the date and time of the wolf or pack presence and the number of times the wolves approached the area. RAG boxes are most effective in smaller pastures (up to 25 hectares), especially during calving and lambing times.

Other Strategies

There are other non-lethal control measures. Many of these methods are more effective on flocks of sheep than on cattle, which mainly benefit from fladry and night-watch shepherding:

- Predator-resistant fences need to be tall and have an underground apron.
- Electric fences can be effective, but the predator animal needs to receive a shock to be conditioned. Fences with five or more alternating hot and ground wires have proven effective and are feasible for small pastures surrounding sheep or llamas.
- Livestock should be kept in well-lit enclosures at night during peak predation times.
- Pasture management means paying attention to times of year and locations of increased predation, and moving livestock to lower incident areas. Rotating livestock over several smaller pastures will increase surveillance by ranchers.
- Scarecrows have short-term effectiveness, and it has been suggested that parking vehicles in areas where losses occur can similarly reduce predation.

- Propane scare cannons produce timed, loud explosions. They need to be moved on a daily basis and fired at regular repeated intervals (with a timer fuse) just before dark and at daybreak unless depredation is occurring during the daytime.
- Radios left playing in a pasture can deter predators; all-night talk shows are ideal programs that wolves dislike. Move radio locations regularly.
- Strobe lights and sirens, controlled by a variable timer that is activated at night with a photoelectric cell, have proven to reduce predation rates in fenced pastures less than 40 hectares or near bedding areas.

However, predators can also be a benefit in agricultural areas, which many ranchers and farmers realize. Damage from ungulates eating or trampling on crops, rubbing antlers on and eating the buds off of trees can be extensive. Beavers in high densities can cause big problems with flooding and water diversion. Wolves preying upon these herbivore populations are a natural mitigation that more and more people recognize. This logic extends to seeing the benefits of other wild dogs, such as coyotes and foxes, preying upon rodent populations that can cause farmers, ranchers and landowners significant grief.

Avoiding livestock depredation is labour intensive, and ranching itself is historically labour intensive as well. Canadian farmers and ranchers are having a more and more difficult time seeing profits with the economic policies of our government on global markets and international trade. Ranchers and farmers find mitigation efforts an extra burden and cost. They have to check herds regularly, ensuring only healthy and non-pregnant cattle are out to pasture. They have to remove cattle from remote leases in the fall, and they have to expect conflict and losses if cattle are placed in remote areas—in cases of negligence, losses from predation are minimally compensated. It is essential for them to bury or remove carrion to avoid attracting or habituating predators to an easy food source.

Attacks on Dogs

Similar to livestock attacks, wolf depredation of small pets is motivated by hunger. Attacks on pet dogs are varied. Small dogs are likely perceived as prey, and any small animal that is taken is typically partially or entirely consumed. Attacks on large dogs seem to be acts of territorial behaviour. It is well known and understood that wolves are territorial by nature. They will aggressively defend their territories against intruding wolves, and to a wolf, a dog is perhaps not much different from another wolf and presents the same offensive threat. A wolf is typically very aggressive toward a large dog discovered in its territory, just as it would be toward a foreign wolf. Conversely, wolves generally respect the territory of a dog and rarely enter a yard or kennel where a large dog is kept. When large dogs are allowed to stray or are taken into the backcountry or let off leash in areas inhabited by wolves, the dog owner is taking a risk.

Nobody wants to see a pet maimed or killed by a wolf. The media subsequently reports on the story and sometimes inflames public prejudices against wolves. There are many practical ways to mitigate wolf attacks on domestic dogs and reduce the risk of injury or death to your pet. While dogs do not necessarily have strong territorial behaviour, wolves by nature definitely do. A dog that does not respect the boundary established by a wolf to delineate its territory faces the same consequences as another wolf or coyote that violates this regulation. Train pets to stay within their own territory—in other words, train dogs to stay in the yard if not kept on a leash. Once a dog runs out of sight, perhaps in pursuit of a rabbit or another dog or even a wolf, the owner will have little chance of reacting quickly enough to that pet's possible encounter with a wolf.

When in wolf territory, backcountry hiking or living in or visiting rural areas with pets, keep in mind these recommendations:

- Keep dogs on a leash when walking or being exercised.
- Keep dogs in a kennel if kept outside of the house—the kennel must have a roof or very high walls (above 1 m).
- Do not allow dogs to stray unattended if let out to relieve themselves.
- If off-leash, always keep the dog in eyesight and near people.
- Recognize fresh wolf signs (tracks, scat or kills) and avoid areas where they are found, or be on heightened alert with pets.
- Feed pets in a secure area if outdoors.

Encounters with People

There are, of course, several things in Ontario that are more dangerous than wolves. For instance, the stepladder.

–J.W. Curran, *The Canadian Wildlife Almanac* (1981)

It is widely accepted in Canada that the wolf is not an aggressive animal toward humans. Unlike the lore of wolves in Europe, from the big bad wolf of fairy tales to the werewolves of mythology and horror stories, wolves in North America have a good reputation. They indeed have suffered much more at the hands of man than man has at the teeth of wolves. However, statements that include the words *never* and *always* are naïve and hazardous. Wolves are wild animals, and each individual wolf is as unique and unpredictable as any individual human being. Through public education, we have learned that wolves are not savage, bloodthirsty animals. Most people have come to admire and respect wolves rather than fear them. However, people are misguided if they do not have any fear of a wild animal. People who attempt to befriend wild animals put themselves at risk of injury and put the animal at risk of being habituated. Habituated animals—animals that are so accustomed to people that they do not avoid people but rather begin investigating opportunities for food handouts or other favours—no longer behave naturally. The more we encroach onto wolf territory, we unintentionally or passively habituate wolves to our presence.

Considering the millions of people who come within close range of a wolf (most likely without realizing, but the wolf is surely aware) in and outside of the national and provincial parks, it is apparent that wolves prefer to avoid us rather than confront us. There have been random cases of aggressive behaviour displayed by wolves toward humans in the past, and it would appear that there are always extenuating circumstances, such as presence of a dog that has agitated the wolf. Wolves do not, however, seem to take advantage of their indisputable ability to cause serious harm to humans. They have the ability to efficiently take down animals the size and stature of moose or bison, breaking leg bones in a single bite or tearing through thick-furred hides; a soft human would be easy prey, but we are simply not regarded as prey by wolves. People have been merely scratched or received minor bites or grazings. The wolves' actions are more demonstrative of reacting to threats, defensive actions or other non-predatory behaviours.

Wolves rarely even fight back when humans attack them. There are videos of biologists working with wolves that are subdued only by a toothless leg trap and a form of pressure to the neck or head. The biologist examines the wolf's teeth and takes blood samples, while the wolf freezes in a pronate, submissive posture. Almost any other animal would be kicking and scratching and fighting for its life. More pathetic are the videos of wolves caught in the same leghold traps; the wolf passively cowers while the hunter or trapper approaches and then shoots it in the head. Mother wolves have not attacked people who have stolen their pups from the den, when otherwise it has been observed that mother wolves fight predators such as bears to the death to protect their young. Early zoo collectors stealing pups from dens described how mother wolves begged for their pups, coming within nose-width of the collectors' legs, but never attacked even for their own whining pups. According to David Mech, a researcher in the High

Arctic captured a wolf pup and took it to his tent; the mother wolf followed him and slept outside his tent all night, listening to the whines of her pup but never once attacking the man. Countless researchers have examined prey carcasses from wolf kills, and the wolf pack always retreats, deferring their valuable, hard-sought prey to people without the aggression they show toward bears or cougars or any other animal that would be so bold as to attempt to usurp a wolf's dinner. John James Audubon describes wolves that were captured in a pit trap by a farmer, who jumped into the pit, severed their leg tendons, pulled them out of the pit and threw them to a pack of dogs. The wolves only cowered from the man and never attempted to defend themselves.

Habituation, however, is a growing concern. In 2006, there was the first human fatality caused by wolves in North America in documented history. It occurred in northern Saskatchewan and has been attributed to habituated wolves. The victim was alone so precise details on the attack are unknown, but forensic experts and biologists confirmed that wolves made the attack. The wolves in the area were habituated to the local garbage dump, which is the case in many northern communities where unfenced, open-air dumps attract wildlife. For example, workers at the Key Lake uranium mine in Saskatchewan, the largest uranium mine in the world, have reported wolf attacks and claim that the wolf packs there have ceased hunting wild prey and have fed exclusively on human garbage for generations. In areas of high industrial activity, habitat loss pushes out natural prey; wolves finding less prey in their territories have found garbage as a food source. There are several cases of human injury from such habituated wolves.

There has unfortunately been a recent human fatality in Canada caused by coyotes: in October 2009, a young woman hiking in Cape Breton Highlands National Park in Nova Scotia was attacked and killed by two coyotes or possibly coyote–wolf hybrids. This event shocked the nation. There had never been such a case, and attacks on adult humans are extremely unusual for either coyotes or wolves, which are otherwise nervous and timid animals around people. Park Superintendent Helene Robichaud said it had been 20 or 25 years since she had even heard of a coyote attack. That this attack was severe enough to be fatal, "It's unusual, it's infrequent, irregular," she told CBC reporters. Bob Bancroft, a retired biologist with the Nova Scotia Department of Natural Resources, stated that a coyote attacking a human is "very unusual and is not likely to be repeated," owing to the animals' inherent shyness. A trapping incentive in Nova Scotia of $20 per coyote tail, considered by some to be a bounty, was announced on April 24, 2010; it is not known at present what effects the bounty will make on coyote population or behaviour, but strong public awareness campaigns have been implemented on how to avoid wildlife (coyote) conflict. Saskatchewan implemented a coyote bounty in November 2009 of $20 for 4 paws; there were 71,000 coyotes harvested compared to an anticipated normal harvest of 26,000. Certain agricultural areas in Saskatchewan where high ground squirrel populations are problematic opted out of the bounty. The bounty ended March 31, 2010 and has not been renewed. After a coyote lunged at a 16-year-old boy, the community group in Osgood, outside of Ottawa, reacted by implementing the Great Coyote Cull Contest, in which successful hunters brought in proof of dead coyotes and were then entered into a draw for a new shotgun.

Any wild animal—from squirrels to birds to deer to wolves to bears—can become attracted and habituated to human garbage and food scraps. To mitigate habituation, people must be responsible with their garbage when visiting or living in wilderness areas. Keep yards tidy, with garbage in containers that are tightly sealed and out of reach of animals. Placing fences around compost piles is also a good idea—though wolves are unlikely to be attracted to the compost, other animals may be, and they could be prey animals of wolves. Do not leave bowls of pet food outside, but feed pets only what they will eat at one feeding and clean up any leftovers.

It is incredibly rare and unusual to have any encounter with a wolf. Recent increases in encounters with habituated wolves (and coyotes) receive considerable media attention, partially because they are so remarkably unusual. While it is important to educate the public that any wild animal has the potential to inflict harm, the perceived threat from wildlife tends to become greatly exaggerated in people's minds. Residents of the Clearwater community in Alberta were surveyed about their perceptions of cougars in the area (Knopff, A.A. 2010). People were asked whether they were comfortable coexisting with cougars and when it is acceptable to shoot a cougar; the responses were medium. The value of cougars was perceived to be high by most respondents, who claimed that they wanted to keep cougars on the landscape. They felt that their chance of interaction was high, regardless of experiences. When residents were asked whether they felt that would have a higher chance of experiencing a cougar attack or being hit by a car, 27% of respondents felt they would have a higher chance of experiencing a cougar attack and 20% felt that the chances of either incident would be equally likely. In the year of this survey, there were 142,592 car accidents with 453 fatalities in Alberta, while only one cougar fatality had occurred in 120 years.

Although it is rare that a wolf would act aggressively toward a dog on a leash or in close proximity to its human owner, there have been exceptions. In these cases, the threat to the wolf was great enough for it to suppress its natural avoidance of people. If a wolf approaches a human with little or no fear, with uncharacteristic boldness, it is becoming habituated to human presence. These wolves need to be reported to the authorities.

Do not act submissive in any way toward a wolf. It is a rare and amazing experience to see a wolf at close proximity, but do not indulge in the experience too long nor encourage the wolf to approach you. Do not try to make friends with the wolf; you are doing it more harm than good. Do not turn your back, but retreat from the wolf's territory. It is probably also a good idea to make the wolf associate its experience with you negatively so that it keeps a healthy fear of people. While respecting the wolf's territory and removing yourself swiftly, try also to scare the wolf away from you. Stand tall, make noise, holler, threaten it with your body language, throw rocks or sticks toward it (not at it—do not injure the animal). In the unlikely case that the wolf persists in approaching you, showing acts of aggression, such as snarling, baring its teeth and continuing to advance, be prepared to defend yourself. Cases of wolf attacks were once unheard of, but we can no longer afford the luxury of making that statement. There have been wolf attacks on people in Canada, mostly with minor injury, but a few have been serious, and one fatal. If a wolf ever attacks you, fight back.

Wolves kept in captivity as pets are another issue, part of the same debate as any non-domesticated animal being captured or born into captivity and subsequently observed—not behaving quite like a pet, but not quite wild. We resist allowing ourselves to anthropomorphize, but we often can't help but consider these animals' behaviours. In human terms, individual animals have been described as unhappy, bored or psychotic. It is prohibited to have a wolf as a pet in most of Canada, though unregulated in the northern territorial communities, where hybrids are also more common. Keeping hybrids as pets is largely prohibited across most jurisdictions, but again, unregulated in parts of the country.

There are hundreds of wolves in zoos around the world, with thousands of pups born in captivity and later sold with uncertain futures. Most modern and responsible zoos have large habitats for wolves, and neuter the adults. According to Busch, there are over 30 wolves in zoos in Canada: Calgary Zoo, Greater Vancouver Zoo, Jardin Zoologique de Quebec,

Magnetic Hill Zoo in Moncton, Metro Zoo in Toronto, Valley Zoo in Edmonton and Zoo Sauvage de Saint-Félicien in Quebec.

Owners of wild wolves have tried to set them free, as did Bill Mason. He documented his "pet" wolves in a couple of documentaries for the National Film Board of Canada in the 1970s. He studied several wolves that he had owned since they were pups, either born into captivity or stolen from their wild dens. The former were tame, but the latter retained a wild distrust and never allowed Mason to handle them. Mason fed his wolves venison: he had carcasses delivered on a regular basis, from a road kill or various other scenarios. The wolves never hunted for their own meals. They were let into a large run for exercise but kept in outdoor kennels at night. Mason began to question their quality of life, and took his wolves up to the Northwest Territories to an area he knew well where he had filmed wild wolves. He released them where he knew caribou were available for hunting. He then camped out and observed to see if the wolves would try to hunt. They didn't, and it became sadly obvious to Mason that they would soon starve; he had to recapture them and take them back to their cages in rural Quebec.

MITIGATING HUMAN IMPACTS ON WILDLIFE

Vocabulary such as *mitigation* is more and more common in conservation jargon. No longer is it realistic to use words such as *prevention*, it seems, when it comes to industrial development. Hunting quotas are probably the only form of human mitigation on wildlife. In my home province of Alberta, I have yet to see a development project (forestry, coal mines, tar sands, oil wells) overturned, only mitigated. Provinces such as BC seem to have a better track record, and celebrate beautiful areas such as Clayoquot Sound. But for the most part, Canada's economy still embarrassingly clings to unsustainable dirty industry and non-renewable resources. What is considered mitigation of human activity these days? Replacing an old-growth forest with a tree farm? Slicing off a mountain top and planting grass afterward? Turning boreal forest into prairie and plunking some semi-domesticated bison on it to graze?

When it comes to predator management, we are much more aggressive. We permit the minimum allowable presence, whereas with human development management we permit the maximum allowable. Wolves and other predators are managed for a minimum "ecological effectiveness." "It is not sufficient for wolves to merely be present; they must be at a certain density or population to be effective in the ecosystem" (Soule et al. 2005). A minimum viable population is a management strategy that mitigates wolf extinction or extirpation while minimizing any hypothetical human inconvenience: lowered hunting quotas, potential for livestock losses, wildlife corridors or habitat reserves that may disallow road, recreational or industrial development, and so on. So, as long as humans are not inconvenienced, wolves can exist.

Hunters and trappers, wolf advocates and wildlife managers have been pitted against each other in situations such as the woodland caribou–wolf controversy when really, all of them would like to see a wildlife system that has ecological integrity. The problem is that way too much forestry, oil and gas and other development, condoned by a government perceived to be in bed with industry, impedes any chance of habitat restoration and, ultimately, caribou survival. Wildlife managers are put in a difficult position, having to manage animals while having little to no influence on the provincial or territorial government protecting habitat.

When game animal populations plummet to levels where human harvest is no longer permitted, hunters can become frustrated by the increased predation by wolves and set their sights on them instead. In most cases the low ungulate population is related to habitat loss, which often goes unchecked. With little data available on wolf status in many parts of their ranges, or on other large predators like the cougar, wolverine and grizzly bear, it often comes down to public perception about wolf status influencing management.

Canada's Mountain Wolves

I can sometimes hear them singing from the hills above Jasper—the dogs without masters, the dogs who are free.
—Ben Gadd, *Handbook of the Canadian Rockies*

The American Cordillera is a massive mountain system that spans North America from Alaska's Brooks Range to the western Sierra Madre in Mexico. It crosses the entire longitude of western Canada with the Mackenzie Mountains, Columbia Mountains and Rocky Mountains. This landscape is scenically spectacular and full of wildlife, including wolves.

Several wolf packs reside in Canada's mountain ranges, with several species of ungulates as available prey: the most abundant, and therefore the main prey, are elk. In more or less sequential order of abundance are bighorn sheep, mule deer, white-tailed deer, moose, mountain goat and a small, threatened population of woodland caribou. Deer are generally outcompeted by elk and therefore have low densities, particularly throughout elk winter ranges. Moose are rare, and bighorn sheep and mountain goats are spatially separated from wolves in the winter but become more preyed upon in the spring, particularly the young. Other predators in the mountains are cougars, coyotes, grizzly bears and black bears.

In Canada's Rockies are three of our country's most iconic national parks: Banff, the second oldest national park in the world and a UNESCO World Heritage Site; Waterton Lakes, connected at the US border to Glacier, forming the International Peace Park and also a UNESCO World Heritage Site; and Jasper. There are many more provincial parks and wildlife areas all along the foothills of both the eastern and western slopes. The Canadian Pacific Railway commissioned artists to paint this landscape, promoting it to bring the first homesteaders out to the West. Those artists not only captured the beauty of Rockies but also became among the most celebrated artists of our nation—the Group of Seven. They established an art form that captured not only the Canadian landscape but also a Canadian identity formed by our connection with nature and wilderness.

Banff National Park is a grand park full of lakes and backcountry hikes, cross-country and downhill ski trails, campgrounds, hotels and a townsite that is by all rights a city. The park is 6641 km^2 and characterized by extreme mountainous topography (including elevations of 1400–3400 m). The climate is characterized by long, cold winters with infrequent warm weather caused by chinook winds, and short, relatively dry summers.

Though hard to believe today, when the first national park in Canada was established in 1885, Banff National Park (originally called Banff Hot Springs Reserve) was conceived as a recreation area for people, where wolves were unwelcome. Wolves were extirpated from Banff and other protected areas by the early 1900s. Parks were void of natural predators. It was not just Banff; even Algonquin Provincial Park, now a wolf haven where tourists flock to hear wolves howl, once had a mandate to remove wolves. According to the Algonquin Wolf Advisory Group, "Following extensive logging of the late 1800s and early 1900s, wolves continue to persist despite considerable effort by Algonquin Provincial Park rangers to eliminate them." In 1909, the superintendent of Algonquin Provincial Park even wrote a magazine article titled, "How Shall We Destroy the Wolf?"

Wolves had not denned in Banff National Park in over 30 years until finally, people's attitudes and conservation policies shifted and wolves were permitted to naturally recolonize in the 1980s: wolves denned again in the Bow Valley of Banff National Park in 1986. There are now approximately 35–40 wolves in Banff National Park. However, they still face a myriad of obstacles and dangers within these "protected areas": 91% of wolf mortality in Banff National Park is human caused. Over the years, there have been losses from legal and illegal hunting, road or rail kill, trapping and predator control. The statistics are not much better in other parks; for example, in Riding Mountain National Park in Manitoba, 78% of wolf mortality was human-caused prior to 1980. Even in Algonquin Provincial Park, the largest protected area for wolves in the world at 7653 km^2, 60% of wolf mortalities are caused by humans.

The towns in and around the Rocky Mountains fragment the valley with their numerous hotels and other tourist facilities, in addition to resident population, community infrastructure and amenities, the national railway and highway system and numerous secondary roads and other human developments (such as ski resorts and golf courses). Although the Bow Valley comprises the best winter range habitat for elk inside Banff National Park, wolves are known to avoid the area owing to the high human development. The Trans-Canada Highway, a four-lane highway running through the national park, and the railway are sinks for wildlife mortality from collisions; wolves from the Bow Valley pack are often killed on the Trans-Canada, as happened in August 2008 when the lead breeding female was killed by a vehicle collision. Wolves regularly cross the Trans-Canada even though it is fenced. The fencing was put up to try to prevent roadkill but in effect just created another barrier between predators and their prey.

Montane is an ecoregion on the lower slopes and valleys above the foothills of the Rockies. Montane valley floors, which are critical winter habitat for ungulates and therefore for their predators as well, exist along major eastern-slope rivers such as the Bow, the North Saskatchewan and the Athabasca; they comprise 2–10% of the entire Rocky Mountain land area. The most human recreational and industrial development is in the montane and the adjacent foothills. Almost three-quarters of logged public land in Alberta is in the foothills. There are somewhere in the number of 30,000 oil and gas–related wells drilled in the foothills. And what the US Forest Service indicates is the maximum acceptable road density for grizzly bear habitat is exceeded by 96% in Canada's Rocky Mountain foothills.

The Ya Ha Tinda is a high-elevation montane grassland, or "mountain prairie," as is the apt and eloquent meaning of the name in the Stoney-Sioux language. It is one of the most pristine and largest rough fescue montane grasslands left in Alberta. The Ya Ha Tinda is also the transboundary system spanning Banff National Park's boundaries into adjacent provincial lands; it is nearly 40 km^2 along the north side of the Red Deer River. There are more wolves in this area than in the parks owing to less human impact.

Yellowstone to Yukon (Y2Y) is a conservation initiative to connect habitat and migratory corridors along the mountain ranges between Yellowstone National Park all the way north to the Canadian Columbia and Mackenzie mountains in the Northwest Territories and the Yukon. It is a habitat corridor 3200 km long by 500–800 km wide, amounting to approximately 1.3 million km^2 of protected area. It includes five states (Montana, Idaho, Wyoming, Oregon and Washington), two provinces (BC and Alberta) and two territories (the Yukon and the Northwest Territories).

The idea for the initiative came from scientists tracking a wolf named Pluie. This five-year-old female grey wolf was radio-collared in Alberta's Peter Lougheed Provincial Park in June 1991. Over the next two years this young wolf was tracked as she traversed a 100,000 km^2 area! She moved through several provinces and states, passing through Banff National Park and Glacier National Park, crossing international borders and trespassing dangerously out of protected areas into hunting zones and onto private property and ranch lands. Pluie was legally shot, still wearing her collar, along with her mate and three pups, near Invermere, BC, in 1993.

This example proves that there is no park or protected area large enough to provide sufficient habitat for far-ranging animals such as wolves, bears and cougars. As they move in search of prey, mates or space that is not in competition with other predators' territories, they are often unprotected. For species that are sensitive to human impact, it is apparent the scattered parks and protected areas are like pieces of confetti on the landscape, and without connection, they cannot offer refuge. Collaboration between organizations and individuals throughout the Rocky Mountain cordillera ecosystem brought the Y2Y vision to fruition. Education programs on the socio-economic benefits and partnerships between various groups are part of the advocacy work. A couple of examples to date of what has been achieved include BC's creation of the 6.5 million hectare Muskwa-Kechika management area and the federal government's announcement of its desire to expand Waterton Lakes National Park. Beginning in 1998, Canadian conservationist Karsten Heuer walked 3400 km—in the company of wolves—along the Rockies on an epic Yellowstone to Yukon hike, campaigning for the identification and management of connective migratory corridors.

REINTRODUCTION OF CANADIAN GREY WOLVES INTO THE UNITED STATES

When the lower United States had nearly eradicated the wolf completely, the last sorry individuals surviving in the Midwest were referred to as outlaws and given bandit names such as Custer Wolf, Three Toes and Mountain Billy. Stories of 150 men—bounty hunters called "wolfers"—being eluded by old Three Toes all end on a celebratory note when he is finally shot near Thunder Butte, South Dakota, in the 1920s. Poor old Three Toes is believed to have been the last wolf in the tri-state area of South Dakota, Wyoming and Montana.

If he was the last wolf, the species had then been completely extirpated from that area.

Then, in 1994, a few conservationists decided to return the wolf to its abandoned ecosystem. It has been a controversial issue, debated ever since. Americans hoping to restore the species to its former habitat took Canadian wolves and transplanted them to parts of Idaho, Wyoming and Michigan. Some wolves survived, particularly the population that stayed within the protected boundary of Yellowstone; but many reintroduced wolves outside of the parks were simply poisoned or shot by angry local residents. These wolves were thrown, ironically, like lambs to wolves.

At the time of the initial reintroductions, those protesting were the Foundation of North American Wild Sheep, Wyoming Woolgrowers, Wyoming Farm Bureau Association, No-Wolf Option and the Cody Chamber of Commerce. The controversy surrounding the wolves' return to the US remains heated today. Wolves are not welcomed by everyone, and even study animals that are collared and monitored within the reintroduction program have been shot. Is it right or ethical to transplant an animal into an area where it is not wanted? An area it has no memory of or history in—and while dealing with the stress of having been moved there, it is being shot at?

The grey wolf has nonetheless reestablished in the United States, both by deliberate translocation and by natural migration. In October 1994, the first deliberate reintroduction took place. Canadian grey wolves from the Alberta–BC Rockies were captured and transplanted into Yellowstone (15 breeding pairs and their pups) and central Idaho (15 yearlings and non-breeding adults). The wolves were monitored by radio telemetry. Some wolves left the protected areas and were shot; more wolves were then captured in Canada and brought into the United States. The population has slowly increased and expanded west into Washington and Oregon.

There are 1550–1750 wolves in Minnesota, about 60 in Wisconsin and upper Michigan, and approximately 12 in Isle Royale. There has been natural recolonization of Canadian wolves into Montana and Washington as well as to New England and New York—as people let their guard down, feeling that the wolf was gone, the wolf slowly tiptoed its way back.

With growing awareness of conservation and natural systems, it was apparent that the loss of the wolf, as well as many other species such as the grizzly and the condor, had left holes in nature's fabric. Over time those holes would fray, losing more and more of the ecosystem's integrity as plants and animals were affected by the missing links in systems where species had co-evolved for thousands of years. Other animals would step into the vacant niches. For example, the coyote has stepped into what was formerly the wolves' territory, but the shoe doesn't quite fit. Coyotes don't take down large livestock—a plus in the eyes of ranchers—but they are readily habituated and come close to urban areas and can prey upon people's pets. In rural areas they can go after smaller livestock such as fowl. Meanwhile, nothing is keeping the deer in check, and their populations are on the rise as they compete with livestock grazing. With few established wolves, there are incidents of wolf–coyote hybridization, leading to new management issues as conservationists determine how to manage this new animal (see Wolf Hybrids, p. 43).

Since the passage of the Endangered Species Act in 1973, Canadian grey wolves have slowly recolonized northwestern Montana. Wolves from Alberta had already naturalized back into Montana, but there was no evidence of breeding wolves until February 24, 1993, when a state employee confirmed a breeding pair of wolves in the Sun River Wildlife Management area, home to nearly 3000 wintering elk. The pair was later tracked by helicopter and the male darted with a tranquilizer. He was 55 kg, the largest wolf captured in the lower 48 states in recent decades. He already had an ear tag

that verified he was a Canadian wolf from BC; he had been captured and tagged as a pup five years before, 50 air miles away from where he was now captured. He had been tagged as part of a wolf study led by University of Montana professors Robert Ream and Dan Pletscher. Pletscher said that after this wolf was tagged in 1988, the pack disappeared and he thought they had been poisoned. If they were, there was at least one survivor. The wolf was now nicknamed Clyde, and his mate Bonnie—outlaws again. Local ranchers were extremely cooperative and allowed the researchers to track the wolves throughout their properties. Two months after Bonnie and Clyde were first observed, four pups were born. The wolves denned and reared their pups "smack in the middle of a pasture with dozens of cattle, including calves"; however, they never once in the study summer attacked the cattle, preying exclusively on mule deer and elk calves. Montana, Idaho and Wyoming now have well-established wolf packs from Yellowstone National Park northwest to the Canadian border. As of 2010, Washington has two confirmed packs, potentially several more, and Oregon has enough regular wolf sightings that they expect to announce resident packs in the near future as well.

INTRINSIC VALUE

The International Union for Conservation of Nature (IUCN) Manifesto on Wolf Conservation states in its first clause of the Declaration of Principles for Wolf Conservation: "Wolves, like all other wildlife, have a right to exist in a wild state. This is in no way related to their known value to mankind. Instead, it derives from the right of all living creatures to coexist with man as part of natural ecosystems."

Due to the elusive nature of wolves, seeing one in the wild is rare and fortunate, a prize beyond the pelt value to any photographer and to those who will share the sight in books and magazines. The wolf has lived through many eras on this continent: an era before humans walked about on these lands, an era when it was part of a pantheon, an era when it was a villain, an era when it was a commodity, and perhaps now, an era when it is just a wolf.

There is a strong industry in the non-consumptive appreciation of wildlife that has been around for years and is growing. For example, Robert Bateman is a Canadian artist whose wildlife paintings honouring nature, including poignant images of the wolf, have been celebrated the world over for decades. Bateman worked three summers in the 1940s at a wildlife research camp in Algonquin, surely listening to those wolves howl. Artists, photographers, birdwatchers, wolf-howling enthusiasts and those who love nature want wolves around and want them protected for future generations to see. Many other people who may never enter a park still believe that wildlife and wild spaces have a right to exist beyond human enjoyment.

A few years ago, a Robert Bateman mural was commissioned for the northern Manitoba city of Thompson. The theme of the mural was the wolf. Completed in 2006, the mural stands 10 stories high and can be seen from a mile away. The mural generated so much public interest in wolves that it soon became apparent that wolves were important and valued. A new wolf park has been proposed to create

habitat for the two captive wolves in the local zoo and a wolf research centre is being proposed, with Thompson positioned to make itself the wolf capital of Canada. There was more wolf art created after the mural was painted. A rock face sculpture of wolves howling at the moon is underway. Forty-nine wolf statues, each 2.3 m tall, have been commissioned by private sponsors and painted by various Manitoba artists; they are positioned around the province with GPS coordinates for a fun wolf "hunt." Ecotourism is already a strong industry in Manitoba with people coming from around the world to see the polar bears in Churchill; now they want to see the wolves too.

Algonquin Provincial Park's first public wolf howl took place on an August evening in 1963. Local researchers modestly announced that they were holding a naturalist program where park wolves were being encouraged to howl, and that visitors could come and listen. They were overwhelmed when 164 cars pulled into the parking lot carrying approximately a thousand visitors showing up for the event. Since that time, 153,600 people have participated in the wolf howl program, with 1500–2000 people attending each event, which take place up to five times per summer. According to program organizers, over 50% of participants are new, with the rest being return visitors. Wolves will often reply to a human wolf call, but people must be sensitive not to do this in the spring when packs may have dens with new pups. A pack will relocate if they hear any wolves (or people sounding like wolves) anywhere near their den; it is stressful, and moving during this vulnerable stage puts the pups at risk.

Many people travel far to come to a place where they may hear "the call of the wild," a familiar phrase synonymous with the call of the wolf. Recorded "music" of wolves howling is popular and can be found in many music stores. Shops in the tourist areas of the Rocky Mountain national parks are full of toys, trinkets, furnishings and clothing with depictions of wildlife. Tourists walk around with hats and t-shirts that bear images of the wolf, like any sports fan wearing their favourite team's jersey. Most people visiting wilderness areas in Canada realize that their chances of seeing a wolf are slim, but they are thrilled to be there just knowing that wolves are around.

If intrinsic value does not sway policy enough, we can speak in economic terms too. An entire additional book could be written on the economic value of ecotourism in Canada, and countless authors and researchers have written on the subject in past decades. Wolves count in both non-monetary and monetary value systems.

Conclusion

The way that wolves are perceived in Canada has been dynamic over time, and increasingly positive by most people. Canadian voices were heard above the hatred in times when wolves were in need of advocacy; these Canadians influenced generations to celebrate and protect the wolf. The advocacy continues today.

Today we live in a country that is strongly identified by its connection to wildlife and wild places. Centuries have passed since the arrival of the first French and English trappers and fur traders, but many Canadians still live on the land, trying to be a part of a system rather than live on the periphery of nature. One of the major recreational activities in Canada is getting out into nature to experience wilderness and see wildlife. Indigenous culture still sees the wolf the same way it did hundreds, perhaps thousands, of years ago; rather than being lost, that paradigm has been shared so that today Canadians of all cultures see animals such as the orca, the grizzly, the Canada goose and, of course, the wolf as totems of our nation. This totemic perspective of wildlife is appreciated and familiar to Canadians, and it is how we present our identity to the rest of the world.

In an era where most large mammalian predators of the world are threatened, at risk or endangered, often critically, wolves have persevered throughout most of their pre-colonial range in Canada—most other large mammals, particularly predators such as bears and cougars, have not fared as well. Biologists and naturalists have taught us not to fear wolves the way we did when fairy tales and horror stories governed our emotions through ignorance. Many hunters and ranchers appreciate the existence of the wolf and realize its importance in maintaining the health of ungulate populations. We have begun to understand the importance of the wolf in Canada's varied and complicated ecosystems. We realize that, even still, science is searching for answers to the many questions we have about wolves. Throughout Canada's great northern forests and expansive subarctic and arctic regions, wolf populations are unknown, only surmised at. We do know that Canada has more wolves than any other country in the world, and this privilege makes us aware that our spectacular wilderness is a defining characteristic of Canada. We are left to ponder, then, what is the related defining characteristic of the people who live in Canada?

Wolves have been put in the unenviable position of being our mirror, guiding our consciences and influencing how we see reality and the natural world. We can look into the amber eyes of the wolf and feel proud or shamed, appreciation or prejudice. If we don't like what we see in that mirror, how shall we react? The wolf does not deserve human hatred, or request human adoration; it has the right alongside every other Canadian—the feathered, furred or finned citizens—to just be. Will we be wise and unselfish enough to afford it that right over the next century that is going to see ever-increasing pressure on our Canadian wilderness?

Management plans often look at wolves pragmatically, with an economic or ecological perspective. But there is a growing awareness toward affording the wolf a purely intrinsic value—a right to exist regardless of its perceived values. Attitudes have become more sophisticated, and in recent decades, hunters, trappers, ranchers, researchers,

artists, conservationists, animal rights defenders and various others have found a common voice in realizing the wolf's inherent right to exist in Canada. The wolf does not and should not have to exist in Canada because it has our permission to do so. The wolf survives in Canada because of its own stamina and perseverance and partially because it has never shown us the hatred we have shown it. Of the millions of humans and thousands of wolves in Canada, there are next to no incidents of wolves attacking humans, while hundreds of thousands of wolves have been killed by humans in the past hundred years.

From the time when settlers and colonialists feared nature, delineated and claimed "Canada" and saw the wolf as a threat and a competitor, we have learned how much nature has forgiven and continues to provide for us. We are emblazoned with a sense of responsibility to give back and protect this adopted land and the creatures that were here much earlier that we were. The last century likely saw the most interesting evolution in Canadian perceptions of wolves; we went from actively and often vengefully hunting and killing wolves to passively listening to them howl. What will this century hold in store for the wolf in Canada?

References

Alberta Forestry, Lands and Wildlife: Fish and Wildlife Division. 1991. Management plan for wolves. *Wildlife Management Planning Series 4.*

Atkinson, K.T. and D.W. Janz. 1994. Effect of wolf control on black-tailed deer in the Nimpkish Valley on Vancouver Island. *Wildlife Bulletin* B-73. BC Ministry of Environment, Lands and Parks, Nanaimo, BC.

Backgrounder on Wolf Management in Ontario. 2005. Ontario Ministry of Natural Resources.

Ballantyne, E.E. 1956. Rabies control programme in Alberta. *Canadian Journal of Comparative Medicine* 20 (1): 21–30.

Bergerud, A.T. and J.P. Elliot. 1986. Dynamics of caribou and wolves in northern British Columbia. *Canadian Journal of Zoology* 64: 1515–1529.

———. 1998. Wolf predation in a multiple-ungulate system in northern British Columbia. *Canadian Journal of Zoology* 76 (8): 1551–1569.

Bergman, C. and T. Mack. 2005. Community oriented wolf strategy: Year 1 progress report June 2003–August 2004. Alberta Sustainable Resource Development, Pincher Creek, AB.

Boyd, D.K., et al. 1994. Prey taken by colonized wolves and hunters in the Glacier National Park Area. *Journal of Wildlife Management* 58 (2): 289–295.

Busch, R.H. 2007. *The Wolf Almanac: A Celebration of Wolves and Their World.* Fitzhenry and Whiteside, Markham, ON, 1995. Reprint, Lyons Press/Globe Pequot Press, USA.

Butler, J. 1994. *Dialog with a Frog on a Log.* Duval House, Edmonton.

Carbyn, L.N. 1989. Coyote attacks on children in western North America. *Wildlife Society Bulletin* 17: 444–446.

———. 2003. *The Buffalo Wolf: Predators, Prey and the Politics of Nature.* Smithsonian Institution Press, Washington.

Caribou in British Columbia; Ecology, Conservation and Management. 2000. British Columbia Ministry of Environment, Lands and Parks.

Carlos, A.M. and F.D. Lewis. *The Economic History of the Fur Trade: 1670 to 1870.* Economic History Association. http://eh.net/encyclopedia/article/carlos.lewis. furtrade.

References

Coleman, J.T. 2004. *Vicious: Wolves and Men in America*. Yale University Press, New Haven, CT.

Crisler, L. 1968. *Captive Wild*. Harper & Row, New York.

Darimont, C.T., T.E. Reimchen, and P. Paquet. 2003. Foraging behaviour by grey wolves on salmon streams in coastal British Columbia. *Canadian Journal of Zoology* 81 (2): 349–353.

Dekker, D. 1997. *Wolves of the Rocky Mountains from Jasper to Yellowstone*. Hancock House, Surrey, BC.

Eder, T. and G. Kennedy. 2011. *Mammals of Canada*. Lone Pine Publishing, Edmonton.

Fox, M.W. 1992 (reprint of the 1980 edition). *The Soul of the Wolf: A Meditation on Wolves and Man*. Lyons & Burford Publishers, New York.

Fox, C.H. and M. Bekoff. 2009. Ethical reflections on wolf recovery and conservation: A practical approach for making room for wolves. In *A New Era for Wolves and People: Wolf Recovery, Human Attitudes and Policy*. Edited by M. Musiani, L. Boitani and P.C. Paquet. University of Calgary Press, Calgary.

Grambo, R. 2008. *Wolf: Legend, Enemy, Icon*. Firefly Books, Richmond Hill, ON.

Gunson, J.R. 1992. Historical and present management of wolves in Alberta. *Wildlife Society Bulletin* 20: 330–339.

Heard, D.C. and J.P. Ouellet. 1994. Dynamics of an introduced caribou population. *Arctic* 47 (1): 88–95.

Hebblewhite, M., et al. 2005. Human activity mediates a trophic cascade caused by wolves. *Ecology* 86: 2135–2144.

Hénault, M. and H. Jolicoeur. 2003. Les loups au Québec: Meutes et mystères. Société de la faune et des parcs du Québec. Direction de l'aménagement de la faune des Laurentides et Direction du développement de la faune.

Jacobs, A. (editor). 2009. *Native American Wisdom: A Spiritual Tradition at One with Nature*. Watkins Publishing, London.

Jickling, B. and P.C. Paquet. 2005. Wolf stories: Reflections on science, ethics, and epistemology. *Environmental Ethics* 27: 115–134, in *A New Era for Wolves and People: Wolf Recovery, Human Attitudes and Policy*. Edited by M. Musiani, L. Boitani and P.C. Paquet. University of Calgary Press, Calgary, 2009.

Jones, K. 2002. *Wolf Mountains: A History of Wolves along the Great Divide*. University of Calgary Press, Calgary.

Kays, R., A. Curtis and J.J. Kirchman. 2010. Rapid adaptive evolution of northeastern coyotes via hybridization with wolves. *Biology Letters* 6 (1): 89–93 (published online September 23, 2009).

Knopff, K.H, A.A. Knopff and M.S. Boyce. 2010. Scavenging makes cougars susceptible to snaring at wolf bait stations. *Journal of Wildlife Management* 74 (4): 644–653.

Knopff, A.A. 2010. Cougars in the backyard: Preserving ecological integrity in developing landscapes. Paper presented at ICCB 2010 International Congress for Conservation Biology.

Lake-Thom, R. 1997. *Spirits of the Earth, A Guide to Native American Nature Symbols, Stories and Ceremonies*. Plume, New York.

Landau, D. (editor). 1993. *The Wolf, Spirit of the Wild*. Nature Company, Berkeley, CA.

Latham, A.D.M. 2009. Wolf ecology and caribou-primary prey–wolf spatial relationships in low productivity peatland complexes in northeastern Alberta. PhD dissertation, University of Alberta. Edmonton.

Lawrence, R.D. 1980. *Secret Go the Wolves*. Ballantine, New York.

———. 1986. *In Praise of Wolves*. Ballantine, New York.

London, J. 1964. *Call of the Wild*. Airmont Publishing Company Inc, New York.

Long, K. 1996. *Wolves: A Wildlife Handbook*. Johnson Nature Series, Boulder, CO.

Lopez, B.H. 1978. *Of Wolves and Men*. Charles Scribner's Sons, New York.

McNay, M.E. 2002. A case history of wolf–human encounters in Alaska and Canada. *Wildlife Technical Bulletin* 13. Alaska Department of Fish and Game.

McIntyre, R. (editor). 1995. *War Against the Wolf: America's Campaign to Exterminate the Wolf*. Voyageur Press, Stillwater, MN.

McTaggart-Cowan, I. 1947. The timber wolf in the Rocky Mountain National Parks of Canada. *Canadian Journal of Research* 25, sect. D.

Mech, L.D. 1988. *The Arctic Wolf: Living with the Pack*. Voyageur Press, Stillwater, MN.

———. 1990. Who's afraid of the big bad wolf? *Audubon* 92 (2): 82–85.

———. 1991. *The Way of the Wolf*. Voyageur Press, Stillwater, MN.

———. 1999. Alpha status, dominance and division of labor in wolf packs. *Canadian Journal of Zoology* 77: 1196–1203.

Mech, L.D. and L. Boitani (editors). 2003. *Wolves: Behaviour, Ecology and Conservation*. University of Chicago Press, Chicago.

Mech, L.D, S.H. Fritts and M.E. Nelson. 1996. Wolf management in the 21st century: From public input to sterilization. *Journal of Wildlife Research* 1 (2): 195–198.

Mech, L.D. and U.S. Seal. 1987. Premature reproductive activity in wild wolves. *Journal of Mammalogy* 68 (4): 871–873.

Miller, F.L. and F.D. Reintjes. 1995. Wolf-sightings on the Canadian arctic islands. *Arctic* 48 (4): 313–323.

Morehouse, A.T. 2010. Venison to beef and deviance from truth. Master's thesis, University of Alberta, Edmonton.

Nelson, R.K. 1983. *The Athabaskans: People of the Boreal Forest*. University of Alaska Museum, Fairbanks.

Nowak, R.M. 2003. Wolf evolution and taxonomy. In *Wolves: Behaviour, Ecology and Conservation*. Edited by L.D. Mech and L. Boitani. University of Chicago Press, Chicago.

Palmquist, J. 2002. The gray wolf in Washington. *Wolf Tracks* 18 (2 and 3).

Pissot, J., C. Mamo and G. Pflueger. 2006. Finding ways to live with wolves in cattle country. *Wildlands Advocate* 14 (2). Alberta Wilderness Association, Calgary.

Plotkin, R. and G. McEachern. 2006. *Uncertain Future: Woodland Caribou and Canada's Boreal Forest*. Canada Parks and Wilderness Society and Sierra Club of Canada, Ottawa.

Rigg, R. 2001. Livestock guarding dogs: Their current use world wide. *IUCN/SSC Canid Specialist Group Occasional Paper No 1 [online]*. http://www.canids.org/occasional-papers/

Robichaud, C.B. and M. Boyce. 2010. Spatial and temporal patterns of wolf harvest on registered traplines in Alberta, Canada. *Journal of Wildlife Management* 74 (4): 635–643.

Runtz, M. 1997. *The Howls of August: Encounters with Algonquin Wolves*. The Boston Mills Press, Erin, ON.

Statistics Canada. 2010. *Fur Statistics 2009 (Catalogue No. 23-013-X)*. Government of Canada, Ottawa.

Schlesier, K.H. 1993. *The Wolves of Heaven: Cheyenne Shamanism, Ceremonies and Prehistoric Origins*. University of Oklahoma Press, Norman, OK.

Schilz, T.F. 1988. The Gros Ventres and the Canadian fur trade 1754–1831. *American Indian Quarterly* 12 (1): 41–56.

Seton, E.T. 1903. *Wild Animals I Have Known*. Manhattan Press, New York. Project Gutenburg ebook, 2009.

———. 1929. *Lives of Game Animals*. Doubleday, New York.

Seip, D.R. 2008. Mountain caribou interactions with wolves and moose in central British Columbia. Alces 44: 1–5.

Steinhart, P. 1995. *The Company of Wolves*. Alfred A. Knopf, New York.

Stelfox, J. 1969. Wolves in Alberta: A history 1800–1969. *Alberta Lands, Forests, Parks, Wildlife* 12: 18–27.

Stone, S.A., et al. 2008. *Livestock and Wolves: A Guide to Nonlethal Tools and Methods to Reduce Conflicts*. Defenders of Wildlife, Washington DC.

Strategy for Wolf Conservation in Ontario. 2005. Ontario Ministry of Natural Resources.

Stronen, A.V. 2007. Mitochondrial DNA (mtDNA) sequence divergence and structure in wolves from Manitoba and Saskatchewan. Report to Parks Canada and Manitoba Conservation's Sustainable Development Innovations Fund (Project #23021), Parks & Wildlife and Ecosystem Protection Branch.

———. 2009. Dispersal in a plain landscape: Wolves in southwestern Manitoba, Canada. PhD dissertation, University of New Brunswick, Fredericton, NB.

Soulé, M.E., et al. 2005. Strongly interacting species: Conservation policy, management and ethics. *Bioscience* 55: 168–176.

Swann, B. (editor). 1996. *Native American Songs and Poems: An Anthology*. Courier Dove Publications, Mineola, NY.

Thayer, H. 2004. *Three Among the Wolves: A Couple and Their Dog Live a Year with Wolves in the Wild*. Sasquatch Books, Seattle.

Theberge, J.B. 1975. *Wolves and Wilderness*. J.M. Dent & Sons Limited, Toronto.

Theberge, J.B., and M.T. Theberge. 1998. *Wolf Country: Eleven Years Tracking the Algonquin Wolves*. McClelland & Stewart, Toronto.

———. 2004. The wolves of Algonquin Park: A 12-year ecological study. *Department of Geography, Publication Series* 56, University of Waterloo, Waterloo, ON.

Timm, R.M., et al. 2004. Coyote attacks: An increasing suburban problem. *Proceedings of the Twenty-First Vertebrate Pest Conference*: 47–57.

United States Department of Agriculture: Animal and Plant Health Inspection Service. 1999 (revision of the 1990 edition). Livestock guarding dogs: Protecting sheep from predators. *Agriculture Information Bulletin* 588.

Urton, E. 2004. Population genetics, foraging ecology and trophic relationships of grey wolves in central Saskatchewan. Master's thesis, University of Saskatchewan, Saskatoon.

Wearmouth, C. 2009. Wolves on the range. *Wild Lands Advocate* 17 (1): 22.

Wilson P.J., et al. 2000. DNA profiles of the eastern Canadian wolf and the red wolf provide evidence for a common evolutionary history independent of the grey wolf. *Canadian Journal of Zoology* 78 (12): 2156–2166.

White, P.J., et al. 2005. Wolf EIS predictions and ten-year appraisals. *Yellowstone Science* 13 (1): 34–41.

The Wolves of Algonquin Provincial Park: A Report by the Algonquin Wolf Advisory Group. 2000. Algonquin Wolf Advisory Group, Ontario.

Websites of Interest

Animal Diversity
animaldiversity.ummz.umich.edu/site/accounts/information/Canis_lupus.html

Canadian Parks and Wilderness Society
cpaws.org

Canadian Species at Risk Public Registry
sararegistry.gc.ca

Canadian National Trappers Association
trapper.ca

Canadian Wolf Coalition
canadianwolfcoalition.com

Clan des Loups d'Amerique de Nord (North American Clan of the Wolves)
(in French and English)
clanloups.com/index_en.html

Defenders of Wildlife
defenders.org

EarthRoots—Wolves Ontario!
earthroots.org/index.php/Wolves-Ontario/wolves-ontario

Field Trip Earth (Mexican wolf range map)
fieldtripearth.org/media_image.xml?object_id=1784&file_id=4184

Fur Council of Canada
furcouncil.com

Fur Institute of Canada
fur.ca

Friends of the Wolf
ecobc.org

Haliburton Forest and Wildlife Reserve Ltd.
haliburtonforest.com/wolf.html

Hinterland Who's Who
hww.ca

International Wolf Center
wolf.org

Northwest Wildlife Preservation Society
northwestwildlife.com

Raincoast Conservation Society
raincoast.org/projects/wolves

Science Behind Algonquin's Animals
sbaa.ca/projects.asp?cn=314

Searching Wolf
searchingwolf.com

Spirit Way
thompsonspiritway.ca

Wildlife Genetics
wildlifegenetics.ca

Wolf Adventure: A Wild Insight (Wolf Centre in Saskatchewan)
wolfechovalley.com

Wolf Country
wolfcountry.net/stories

Wolf Song Alaska
wolfsongalaska.org

Earthroots Wolves Ontario! Project
wolvesontario.org

Wolf Web
wolfweb.com/history2.html

Y2Y: Yellowstone to Yukon Conservation Initiative
y2y.net

Government Statistics and Reports on Wolves

British Columbia
env.gov.bc.ca/fw

Alberta
srd.alberta.ca

Saskatchewan
www.environment.gov.sk.ca

Manitoba
gov.mb.ca/conservation/wildlife

Ontario
mnr.gov.on.ca

Quebec
gouv.qc.ca/portail/quebec/pgs/commun/portrait/geographie/climat/faune/?lang=en

Newfoundland and Labrador
www.env.gov.nl.ca/env/wildlife

Nunavut
env.gov.nu.ca

Northwest Territories
enr.gov.nt.ca

Yukon
environmentyukon.gov.yk.ca/wildlifebiodiversity

Washington Department of Fish and Wildlife
wdfw.wa.gov/conservation/gray_wolf/

Montana Fish, Wildlife & Parks: Wolf Program
fwp.mt.gov/wildthings/management/wolf/

Idaho Fish and Game Wolf Management
fishandgame.idaho.gov/cms/wildlife/wolves/

US Fish and Wildlife: Western Gray Wolf
fws.gov/mountain-prairie/species/mammals/wolf/

The Wolves and Moose of Isle Royale
isleroyalewolf.org/wolfhome/home.html

About the Author

Erin McCloskey spent her formative years observing nature from atop her horse while growing up in the countryside of rural Alberta, Canada. She received her BSc with distinction in environmental and conservation sciences, majoring in conservation biology and management from the University of Alberta. An active campaigner for the protection of endangered species and spaces, Erin has collaborated with various NGOs and been involved in numerous endangered species conservation projects around the world. She worked in Italy for several years, as co-author/editor for the *Green Volunteers* guidebook series, managing editor of *The International Journal of Applied Kinesiology* and text author for large-format books on Canada, Ireland and Hawaii for White Star Publishing. After spending time in Argentina, she authored *The Bradt Travel Guide to Argentina*, now in its second edition. She has also written for various magazines, including *Geographical* in the UK. Erin has edited and written several nature guides for Lone Pine Publishing; her recent *Bear Attacks* books study the intricacies of human–wildlife conflict in the US and Canada.